Kids'

TRAVEL GUIDE

TO THE
LORD'S PRAYER

Group
Loveland, Colorado

Group's R.E.A.L. Guarantee to you:

This Group resource incorporates our R.E.A.L. approach to ministry—one that encourages long-term retention and life transformation. It's ministry that's:

Relational
Because learner-to-learner interaction enhances learning and builds Christian friendships.

Experiential
Because what learners experience through discussion and action sticks with them up to 9 times longer than what they simply hear or read.

Applicable
Because the aim of Christian education is to equip learners to be both hearers and doers of God's Word.

Learner-based
Because learners understand and retain more when the learning process takes into consideration how they learn best.

Kids' Travel Guide to the Lord's Prayer
Copyright © 2003 Group Publishing, Inc.

Visit our Web site: **www.grouppublishing.com**

Credits
Contributing Authors: Gwyn D. Borcherding, Teryl Cartwright, Jennifer Nystrom, and Larry Shallenberger
Editor: Amy Nappa
Creative Development Editor: Karl Leuthauser
Chief Creative Officer: Joani Schultz
Copy Editor: Dena Twinem
Art Director: Kari K. Monson
Print Production Artist: Stephen Beer
Illustrator: Steve Duffendack
Cover Art Director/Designer: Bambi Eitel
Cover Illustrator: David Sheldon
Production Manager: Peggy Naylor

ISBN 0-7644-2524-2
10 9 8 7 6 5 4 3 2   12 11 10 09 08 07 06 05 04
Printed in the United States of America.

Table of Contents

An Introduction to the Travel Guide

What is prayer? Is it a magic wand we wave in front of God to get him to turn events and situations to our advantage? Is it simply a conversation? Is it worship? Is it for adults or children or both? Why, when, and how should we talk to God?

Jesus gave a guide to help answer these questions in Matthew 6, what we now call the Lord's Prayer. Many churches recite this passage on a weekly basis, and it's often required memory work for children. But memorizing and reciting don't ensure that children understand the concepts behind these verses. Concepts such as the holiness of God, God's provision, the importance of forgiving as well as being forgiven, and so on.

This guidebook digs deeper into the concepts behind the Lord's Prayer. It helps children not only learn the words to this prayer, but what those words mean and how they apply to the lives of children (and adults) today. Through these lessons children will discover that prayer is more than recitation or a wish list. It's part of a vital relationship with God. What a joy to be part of their journey!

Kids' Travel Guide to the Lord's Prayer was designed to be applicable to kids in grades K–5. Following a look at what prayer is and how we should pray, the lessons explore each phrase of the Lord's Prayer, finishing with a review and a final lesson assuring children that God answers every prayer.

During this thirteen-week course, each child will complete a **Travel Journal**. The Travel Journal will serve as a keepsake so that the concepts behind the Lord's Prayer become written upon kids' hearts and lived out in their everyday experiences.

The **Pathway Point** is the central concept that children will explore and apply to their lives. The **In-Focus Verse** is either the Bible verse with a specific section of the Lord's Prayer, or a verse that summarizes the concept behind the Pathway Point. A **Travel Itinerary** introduces the lesson and explains how the lesson will impact the lives of children.

Please read each lesson thoroughly, and make a model for the crafts before class. If you do, your lessons will flow much more smoothly. The time recommendations are only guidelines. They will change according to how many are in your group, how prepared you are, and how much help you have. Choose activities or adapt them based on the size of your group and the time you have during your class.

Each lesson starts with a **Departure Prayer**. These are creative prayer activities that help introduce the topic and focus children on God. **Tour-Guide Tips** are helps for the teacher, and **Scenic Routes** provide more creative options.

First-Stop Discoveries introduce the children to the concepts behind each section of the Lord's Prayer. The **Story Excursions** are Bible stories or Scripture passages that illustrate a prayer or Bible truth to support each concept. Kids will experience these stories in creative ways, and the stories will give your class variety. Choose what you think will best meet your children's needs. The activities in **Adventures in Growing** lead the children into further application of the point. Each week, ask the children if they had opportunities to pray or demonstrate the previous week's concept in their own lives. This will be an important faith-growing time.

Souvenirs are photocopiable paper activities. Have children collect these and keep them in a notebook or folder. When your study on the Lord's Prayer is complete, each child will have a Travel Journal keepsake to use as a reminder of all he or she has learned. Each lesson closes with a **Home Again Prayer**, which offers a time of commitment and a time to ask God to direct kids' lives.

Any time during your lesson, read the **Fun Fact** section to kids. These provide examples of the lesson's point from familiar and not-so-familiar facts.

Exploring the Lord's Prayer will be a blessing to both you and the children in your class. May God bless you as you help children know God through prayer.

What Is Prayer?

Pathway Point: 🌑 God wants us to talk to him.

In-Focus Verse: "Do not be anxious about anything, but in everything, by prayer and petition, with thanksgiving, present your requests to God" (Philippians 4:6).

Travel Itinerary

God desires to have a relationship with each of us, and an important part of any relationship is communication. God has established prayer as a means for us to communicate with him. Through prayer, we can praise God, ask for forgiveness, thank God for all he's done, and let our requests be made known to him. Prayer allows us to open our hearts to God and let him know our innermost thoughts and desires.

Children are eager to communicate with anyone who will listen to them, but they often feel adults don't care about their thoughts, concerns, and opinions. Use this lesson to teach your children that God wants us to talk to him and gives us many examples of prayer in the Bible. Celebrate with them the joy of communicating with God.

DEPARTURE PRAYER (up to 5 minutes)

Before you pray remind the children that they can talk to God as they would their best friends. God wants to hear what each person has to say. Invite each child to thank God for one good thing that happened in the past week.

Then pray: **Dear Lord, thank you for loving us and hearing us when we pray. Help us to learn to talk to you every day, in every situation. Thank you for answering our prayers and helping us to please you. We love you and praise you for all you've done. Amen.**

1st STOP DISCOVERY (15 minutes) **An Invitation**

This activity emphasizes God's love for each child and his desire to communicate with us.

TOUR GUIDE TIP The activities in this book have been designed for multi-age groups. Select from the activities, or adapt them as needed for your class.

TOUR GUIDE TIP How can we teach children about prayer without actually taking time to pray? If you don't have enough time to pray, you don't have enough time to teach! Fight the temptation to dive into the lesson without asking God for his wisdom. Spending a few minutes in prayer can make the difference between wasting your time and watching it produce much fruit. God will give you wisdom to teach as you ask him for it (James 1:5).

Items to Pack: construction paper, crayons or markers, bright and colorful stickers

Ask: • When have you been invited to something fun, like a birthday party, wedding, or other special event?

• How did you know you were invited?

• What do invitations look like? What do they say?

Say: God has invited each of us to spend time with him and talk to him. 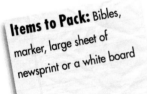 God wants us to talk to him! When we talk to God, it's called prayer. Let's make invitations from God, inviting us to talk to him.

Set out the construction paper, markers or crayons, and colorful stickers. Have each child make an invitation to give to a different child in the class. Let children draw names so they'll each know who to make an invitation for. The invitation should be from God, inviting the child to come and talk to God. Let kids fill in the remaining information as follows:

Time: any time!

Place: any place!

Date: any day!

Remind kids that this is God's personal invitation for a special visit, so they should work to make the invitation as nice as possible. When the invitations are finished, have children deliver them to each other.

Ask: • When you have something important or exciting that you want to share with a friend, how do you usually communicate with him or her?

• Do you need to send a special invitation to talk with your friend?

• How would you feel if every time you had something to talk about with your friend you had to make an appointment or send an invitation?

Say: We don't need an invitation to talk to God. 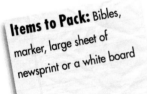 God wants us to talk to him. When we talk to God, it's called prayer, and today we're going to be learning more about what prayer is.

SCENIC ROUTE →

Borrow a book of sample invitations from a stationery shop. Let children look at all the fancy and expensive invitations for inspiration as they make their own.

Items to Pack: Bibles, marker, large sheet of newsprint or a white board

STORY EXCURSION (15 minutes)
ABCs of Prayer

Children will consider reasons why people prayed in the Bible, and reasons why we pray today.

Preparation: Boldly print the letters of the alphabet down the left margin of the newsprint or white board, and place it where children can easily see it.

Open your Bible to Luke 11 and read verse 1 aloud.

Ask: • Why did the disciples need to be taught how to pray?

• Do we need to be taught how to pray? Why or why not?

• What do you think prayer is?

Say: The Bible gives us hundreds of examples of prayers. One prayer from the Bible that many people know is called the Lord's Prayer. We're going to spend the next weeks learning about this prayer. But first, let's look in the Bible to find a few other prayers. We can see why people prayed and what they said in their prayers. This will help us understand more about what prayer is.

Have children form five groups. Be sure that each group has a Bible.

Assign each group one of the following Scriptures, and have the children read the verses together and determine why the person was praying.

Group 1: Genesis 24:12-14

Group 2: 1 Kings 3:7-9

Group 3: Acts 9:36-42

Group 4: Daniel 9:4-5

Group 5: Mark 6:41

Allow several minutes for children to read and discuss. Then ask each group to report why the person in their passage was praying. As they report, write their answer beside the letter of the alphabet that corresponds with the first letter of their answer. For example, Group 1 might answer "guidance," so you would write this beside the letter *G* on your alphabet list. Group 2 might say "wisdom," so this would go beside the letter *W*. Groups may have more than one answer, they may use a short phrase for their answer, and there may be several answers for some letters of the alphabet.

After each group has reported, say: **Let's fill in all the blank letters now. Think of other reasons you or other people you know pray that begin with the letters we still have available.**

Have the class work together to complete the alphabet. Your list might include Ask God for something, Blessing, Confession, Direction, and so on.

Say: **Wow! This is a wonderful list. It shows us there are so many reasons to pray to God. Our list also helps us see that prayer is more than just saying thanks to God before we eat, or more than asking God for a new bike. It's a special way of communicating everything about our lives with God. And best of all,** ◐ **God *wants* us to talk to him! Let's read about one more reason we can pray.**

Read Philippians 4:6 aloud, and ask what this verse teaches us about prayer. Then say: **God doesn't want us to worry about things. God wants us to tell him what's going on in our lives and let him take care of it. Let's say this verse aloud together.**

TOUR GUIDE TIP
If you have adult or teen helpers in your class, ask them to join different groups and help the groups locate and read their assigned verses.

TOUR GUIDE TIP
You may want to write these verses on slips of paper ahead of time to make it easier for children to refer to them.

FUN FACT
Our alphabet has twenty-six letters. The Cambodian alphabet has more letters than any other language. Want to guess how many? Seventy-two letters!

TOUR GUIDE TIP
Here's help on the difficult letters. Q: Quiet heart or Quest for help. X: eXcitement for what God has done or eXpress praise. Y: Yearning to know God or saying Yes to God. Z: Zeal for God or Zillions of things to thank God for. Bring along a dictionary or thesaurus for extra ideas.

Say the verse aloud several times, letting children repeat each phrase. Then say: **The Bible makes it clear that**  **God wants us to talk to him. It's great to know that God cares about us enough to listen to us all the time!**

Items to Pack: paper, pencils

ADVENTURES IN GROWING

(15 minutes)
Preferred Communication

Children will consider ways we communicate with people and ways we can communicate with God.

Have children stay in their groups from the previous activity, and assign each group one of the following forms of communication: sign language, e-mail, letters, telephone, talking face to face. Ask group members to tell each other jokes within their groups, while only using their assigned method of communication. Give the following directions to the various groups:

Sign language group: Only use hands and gestures to communicate. No sounds or lip movement allowed.

E-mail group: Sit back-to-back and write messages on paper, then hand them to others in the group without making eye contact or speaking aloud.

Letters group: Write messages on paper, and silently deliver to others in group.

Telephone group: Sit back-to-back and talk without making eye contact.

Talking face to face group: Converse normally.

After children have communicated jokes for several minutes in this manner, have them sit in their groups and communicate normally as they continue this activity.

Say: **Think of at least two reasons your group's kind of communication is good and at least two reasons this kind of communication is not good. For example, you can use sign language in places where you're supposed to be quiet, like a library, but you can't use sign language to talk on the phone.**

Allow a few minutes for discussion, then have each group report its answers.

Ask: • **If you had to choose only one of these ways of communicating, which one would it be and why?**

• **Which of these ways can we use to communicate with God?**

• **Which form of communication is easiest for you to use to talk with your friends? your parents? God?**

• **Which of these ways of communicating will you use to share what's on your mind with God this week?**

Say: **God doesn't care how we communicate with him. We can write,**

FUN FACT

Everyone knows that Alexander Graham Bell invented the telephone. But who invented the phone booth? Bell's assistant, Thomas Watson. Apparently he shouted so loudly into the phone that his landlady complained. After experimenting a bit, Watson created a wooden booth to use when he was talking on the phone.

speak, or even think what we want to communicate to God, and God hears us and understands us. And God never gives us a busy signal or says the words in our letters aren't spelled right or tells us to come back later when he's not busy. God hears our prayers any time, any place, and any day. ◗ God wants us to talk to him so he's made it easy for us to pray!

(5 minutes)
God's Listening Ears

Children will use a rhyme with hand motions to remind them that they can always talk to God.

Say: In Isaiah 30:19b, the Bible says, "How gracious he will be when you cry for help! As soon as he hears, he will answer you." ◗ God wants us to talk to him. He's ready to hear our every word. Let's learn a poem to remind us that we can pray any time and God will hear us.

Lead the kids in the following rhyme, doing the hand motions and letting children repeat the words and motions.

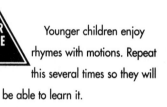
Younger children enjoy rhymes with motions. Repeat this several times so they will be able to learn it.

God is always ready to hear *(cup hands to your ears)*

Words we speak that are sincere. *(Put hand over your heart.)*

He will listen to every prayer *(fold hands as in prayer)*

Any time and anywhere. *(Spread arms to indicate large area.)*

God pays attention to every word *(cup hand to ear again);*

Nothing we say will go unheard. *(Shake head from side to side.)*

So talk to God both night and day *(cup hands around mouth)*

And close beside him you will stay. *(Wrap arms around self as if in a hug.)*

 (10 minutes)
Prayer Journal

Children will record prayers and keep track of God's answers over time.

Items to Pack: "Prayer Journal" handouts (p. 13), pencils or pens

Say: We're going to be learning about prayer for several weeks. Let's start keeping track of what we're praying about, and see what God does in our lives and in the lives of others through these prayers.

Give each child a "Prayer Journal" handout, and make pens or pencils available. Ask children to write or draw at least two things they want to pray about this week, and include the date. Have older children help younger ones who cannot write. Explain that each week kids can add to this list, and they can also note how God answers their prayers over the coming weeks.

If you like, have children glue or tape their invitations to the front of their Travel Journals as a constant reminder that God is inviting them to talk to him.

TOUR GUIDE TIP

If your class is large (or your ceiling is low) you may need to create several towers or even a pyramid of prayer.

TOUR GUIDE TIP

Consider having children write the names and requests of their partners in their Travel Journals. During your next class, let kids check with their partners for updates on these prayers.

SCENIC ROUTE →

Have kids write their names on the back of their Prayer Journal pages, writing the letters down the left margin. Then have them refer to the ABC list created earlier and write reasons to pray that match the letters of their names. This adds a personal dimension to praying!

HOME AGAIN PRAYER

(10 minutes)
Tower of Prayer

This activity becomes a visual prayer.

Preparation: Cut poster board or heavy paper into 4x4 squares. You will need two squares per child.

Give each child two squares. Have the children write or draw a picture of something they would like to talk to God about. It can be something they're thankful for, something they're concerned about, or a visual expression of praise.

As children complete their artwork, invite them to take turns taping their squares to the wall, starting down low near the floor, placing one on top of the other to create a tower of prayer. As you watch the tower grow, notice all the different things the children want to pray about to God. Explain to kids that this is a visual reminder of all the reasons we have to pray.

Say: **Our tower is tall, but it's not how high it is that matters. Our prayers reach God no matter how big or small they are.**

When the tower is complete, have children form pairs. Have children share with their partners about the blocks they created for the tower. Then ask children to sit down together and pray for each other. After a couple of minutes, close the time with this prayer:

Dear God, thank you so much for loving us and for listening to our prayers. We're glad that you want us to talk to you. Help us to talk to you every day this week, no matter what's going on in our lives. Amen.

Prayer Journal

Place this page in the front of your Travel Journal. Use it to keep track of your prayers for the upcoming weeks.

Date	My Prayer	God's Answer

"Do not be anxious about anything, but in everything, by prayer and petition, with thanksgiving, present your requests to God" (PHILIPPIANS 4:6).

How Should I Pray?

(Matthew 6:5-8)

Pathway Point: ◔ The Bible helps us know how to pray.

In-Focus Verse: "Devote yourselves to prayer, being watchful and thankful" (Colossians 4:2).

Travel Itinerary

The idea of talking to God, the creator of the universe, can seem a bit intimidating. How do we approach God? What do we say? What should our attitude be?

Most children are just beginning to consider how communication with God makes a difference in their lives and the lives of others. To some, prayer is a ritual that they do before a meal or at bedtime and it involves little personal interaction. Others may have memorized prayers, but don't know how to share their own thoughts with God. Still others have heard adults pray, yet aren't comfortable talking to someone they can't see.

Use this lesson to show children that through the Bible God helps us know how to pray. As they look to examples from God's Word, they can see that it's the simple and honest prayers that mean the most to God.

DEPARTURE PRAYER
(up to 5 minutes)

Let your kids know that they don't need to use big words or eloquent speech to talk to God. It's more important that we come to God with the right attitude. As you pray today, have the children close their eyes and give a "thumbs up" with their hands to symbolize they're talking to God with a right attitude.

Say: **Dear God, thank you so much for loving us and hearing our prayers. Thank you for the Bible and that it helps us know how to talk to you. Help us to come to you with the right attitudes. Amen.**

1st STOP DISCOVERY A Cup of Cold Water
(15 minutes)

This activity lets children discover the importance of following directions.

Preparation: Cover the sides of one canister of drink mix with paper so the directions cannot be seen. Put one pitcher of water in front of the children. Place the second canister of drink mix and pitcher of water out of sight.

TOUR GUIDE TIP — The activities in this book have been designed for multi-age groups. Select from the activities, or adapt them as needed for your class.

SCENIC ROUTE → Play the CD *Pray* by Rebecca St. James (ForeFront) for background music during some of your activities.

Items to Pack: 2 pitchers of water, cups, 2 canisters of drink mix, measuring spoons, large spoon, paper, tape

14

Say: **I'm going to make us something to drink. I need you all to tell me how to make this stuff.**

Hold up the covered canister. Without removing the cover, have children give you their best guesses as to how to mix a pitcher of the drink. If necessary, let them vote for the amount to add, how long to stir, and so on. After you've done as they suggest, pour a small amount into each cup, and let children taste it.

Ask: • **Does your drink taste like it should? Is it too strong or not strong enough?**

Bring out the second canister and pitcher, and read the directions aloud. Have one or two children help you follow the directions and make a new pitcher of drink. Give each child a taste.

Ask: • **Does this drink taste any better?**

• **How important was it for us to have directions?**

• **What are other times when it helps to have the directions?**

• **Have you ever had something go wrong because you didn't follow the directions? If so, what happened?**

• **Have you ever seen or heard of directions on how to pray? If so, what are they?**

Say: **Sometimes we think we're doing the right thing until we read the directions. It's a good thing** ⬬ **the Bible helps us know how to pray! It gives us the directions we need. In Jesus' time there were many people who thought they knew how to pray. They thought it was important to use big words and impress other people while they were praying. Jesus said that was the wrong way to pray! Let's see what the Bible says about this.**

Read Matthew 6:5-8 aloud.

Ask: • **What directions does Jesus give for prayer?**

• **Do you think these directions are important? Why or why not?**

• **Do you think we should only pray when we're alone? Why or why not?**

Say: **These words of Jesus remind us that when we pray it's important to have the right attitude. We should not be praying to bring attention to ourselves or to ramble on and on. Instead, we should be honest with God about what's going on in our lives and share that with him. There's a Bible story that can help us understand this more.**

TOUR GUIDE TIP

This activity will have more impact if you clearly do not make the drink according to the directions. Side with the children who suggest that you add either a lot or just a little of the powdered mixture to the water so that when you later follow the directions the advantage of doing so will be obvious.

FUN FACT

Sometimes odd items have directions on them. Do you need directions to know how to use a bar of soap? to know how to use toothpaste? to know how to open a jar? Many of these items come with directions! Ask kids to help you think of things that we don't need directions to use—but that still come with directions.

STORY EXCURSION (15 minutes)
Attitude Is Everything

Kids will explore the parable of the Pharisee and the tax collector.

Choose two volunteers. One child will be a Pharisee and hold the big "law book." The other will be a tax collector and hold the bag of "money." Open your Bible to Luke 18 and tell the kids this story comes from the Bible.

Say: **Some people in Bible times thought they were holier than others and looked down on others. Jesus told them this story.**

Two men went up to the Temple to pray. Invite your two volunteers to join you at the front of the room. **One was a Pharisee.** Have your "Pharisee" step forward and bow to the class. **He knew a lot about laws.** Have the Pharisee hold up the law book. **He was very puffed up and proud because of what he knew and how he acted in front of other people.** Have your Pharisee stand very proudly as if he or she is very important. **Everyone thought the Pharisee was important.** Have the class "ooh" and "aah" because they admire the Pharisee.

The other person was a tax collector. Have the "tax collector" step forward and hold up his moneybag. **Everyone hated tax collectors because they were dishonest and greedy and stole from others.** Have the class "boo" the tax collector.

Both of these men had come to the Temple to pray. The Pharisee stood up and prayed about himself. He said "God, I thank you that I am not like other men who are robbers and evildoers, or even like that man over there. Have the Pharisee point to the tax collector and make a disgusted face. **The tax collector! I do everything right. I am so good!"** Pat the Pharisee on the back and have everyone cheer for him or her.

But the tax collector stood far away from the Pharisee. Have the tax collector do this. **The tax collector was ashamed of all the wrong things he'd done. He wouldn't even look up to heaven when he prayed. He kept his eyes on the ground and beat his chest in despair.** Have your tax collector kneel down, look at the ground, and beat his or her chest. **The only thing he could pray was "God, have mercy on me for I am a sinner!"** Have the class remain silent for several seconds to think about the actions of the two men. Then thank your actors and have them return to their seats.

Ask: • **Which prayer do you think pleased God? Why?**

Say: **Jesus went on to tell the people that the tax collector was the one who went home forgiven because he was humble. The Pharisee only wanted to praise himself instead of God.**

After the story, have the kids form pairs or trios and discuss the following questions. Let children discuss each question for one minute, then have one or two groups report their answers before moving on to the next question.

• How do you think the tax collector felt when he went up to the Temple to pray at the same time as the Pharisee?

• What do you think Jesus was trying to teach us with this story?

• What kind of attitude should we have when we pray?

• What's more important, what we say to God or the attitude we have when we say it? Why?

Say: Jesus told this story in the Bible so that we could understand how we should talk to God. The Bible helps us know how to pray.

ADVENTURES IN GROWING

(15 minutes)
The Way Kids Pray
Children will dig in to the Bible to discover more directions on prayer and create signals to remind them of these directions.

Items to Pack: Bibles

Say: Since the Bible helps us know how to pray, let's look at a few more verses that give us directions about prayer. We're going to find out how the Bible says all of us, even kids, should pray.

Have children form two groups. Say: I'm going to read a verse out loud. Then I want each group to do two things. First, decide what this verse tells us about prayer, or what directions it gives us. Then work together to make up a motion or signal to represent this so we can remember this direction.

Read 1 Timothy 2:8 aloud, then let groups discuss and create a motion or signal for this verse. After one or two minutes, have each group share its answer and its signal.

Do this again with each of the following verses, letting the groups take turns going first after each round of discussion and signal creating.

• Acts 27:35

• 1 Thessalonians 5:17

• James 5:16

• Colossians 4:2

Go back and read two or three of the verses again, and see if kids remember the signals they created. Then ask:

• How do these verses help you know how to pray?

• Do you think these directions will work for kids or just for grown-ups? Explain your answer.

• How can you use these signals to remind each other to pray God's way?

Say: **Our theme verse for today is Colossians 4:2. Let's say that one out loud together and do the signals for it one more time.** Read Colossians 4:2 and do the motions with the kids. Say: **God wants us to talk to him so much that the Bible says we should be devoted to praying.**

Ask: • **What does the word "devoted" mean to you?**

• **How much time should a person pray if he or she is devoted to prayer?**

• **How much time are you willing to spend in prayer each day this week?**

• **What's a signal that could remind you to pray this week?**

Have each child think of a signal that will remind him or her to pray. For example, each time a child flips on a light switch, that could be a reminder to pray. Other signals might be hearing a fire engine's siren, tying a shoe, hearing a phone ring, or whatever other signal kids can think of. Have children share their signals with two or three others as a way of saying they'll be devoted to prayer this coming week.

SOUVENIRS → (10 minutes)
My Prayer Place

Kids will consider places they can pray and what they might say at each place.

Say: **One thing Jesus said was that it's a good idea to have a private place to pray. This lets us focus on talking to God and not be distracted by others around us. Let's look at these pictures of this home and think about where we could find a prayer place, and what we could pray about while we're there.**

Have kids look at the pictures and choose one or two places they could pray in their own homes. Ask kid to use the markers or crayons to personalize that area of the handout and to write one or two things they could pray about while in that location. Have older children help younger ones with writing.

HOME AGAIN PRAYER (5 minutes)
Directed to Pray

Children will review what they've learned as they talk to God.

Have the children form a circle. Explain that you're going to close the time in prayer, and as you say words that remind them of what the Bible says about prayer, they should do the signals or hand motions they created earlier. Children may be triggered to do motions by various words, so everyone may not be doing the same motions at the same time.

Pray: Dear God, thank you for giving us the Bible to show us how to pray. Help us to come to you with the right attitudes, without being angry or fighting with others. Help us to confess our sins and to pray for each other. We want to express thanks to you and be devoted to talking to you. In Jesus' name, amen.

Give kids time to write in their Prayer Journals, updating prayer requests, praises, and answers to prayer. Also encourage kids to check in with their prayer partners from last week to see how God has answered prayers since they were last together.

My Prayer Place

"Devote yourselves to prayer, being watchful and thankful" (COLOSSIANS 4:2).

Our Father in Heaven
(Matthew 6:9a)

Pathway Point: ◗ God is our heavenly Father who hears our prayers.

In-Focus Verse: "This, then, is how you should pray: 'Our Father in heaven...' " (Matthew 6:9a).

Travel Itinerary

It's interesting that Jesus began his model prayer with "Our Father." All the disciples knew that Jesus was God's Son, but this phrase verified the fact that we're all God's children. When we address God as "Our Father in heaven," we are personalizing our conversation, not just praying to some unknown being, but actually praying to *our Father.*

All children know what a father is, but not all of the children in your class will have healthy relationships with their earthly fathers. And even the child with the best father will not be able to grasp the greatness of knowing God as a father. It's beyond our comprehension! What a joy to communicate to children the great love that God, their Father, has for them.

| DEPARTURE PRAYER | (up to 5 minutes) |

Before you pray, have the children think of a person who loves them, such as a parent or grandparent. Have children form pairs and share who the person is, and what that person does that lets the child know he or she is loved. Allow two minutes for sharing, then say: **God loves you even more than the person you just shared about. One way we know God loves us is that he hears us when we pray. God also loves us so much that he wants to be our heavenly Father. When Jesus taught his disciples how to pray, he began the prayer by saying, "Our Father." We can begin our prayers that way too.** Have children repeat this prayer after you.

Our Father, we're thankful that you love us and hear us. Amen.

TOUR GUIDE TIP Be sensitive to the fact that some children have no relationship or poor relationships with their fathers. Avoid broad statements such as "All our dads love us," or "Everyone has a father who loves him or her."

SCENIC ROUTE → As children arrive, have paper and crayons or markers available for them to draw a picture of what they think God looks like. This will give you a good idea of what your students' perception of God is.

Items to Pack: 7 sheets of paper, marker, Bible

(15 minutes)

1st STOP DISCOVERY

Your Honor?

This activity helps kids consider the honor it is to call God "our Father."

Preparation: Boldly print the following titles of people in authority on the papers, writing one title per paper: King, President, Principal, Police Officer, Judge, Coach, God.

Choose seven children, and have each child hold one of the signs. Introduce each child, one at a time, introducing "God" last. After each introduction, ask:

• **What's something you might need to talk to this person about?**

Choose two or three children to approach the child you've introduced and ask this child a question as they would if that child really was a police officer, judge, and so on. Choose different children each time so everyone has a turn to participate.

Ask: • **If you needed to talk to this person in real life, would you feel nervous? Why or why not?**

• **Would this person care enough about you to listen to you and answer you? Why or why not?**

• **If you talked to this person, how would you address him or her?**

• **If this person was your close friend or your parent, then how would you address him or her?**

Say: Some people in authority don't have time to listen to us. Even if we give them a lot of respect and address them with respectful names, they don't always listen or answer our concerns. But God does! Even though God is the most powerful person of all, we can call him our Father. And like most dads, God our Father listens to us. In fact, God listens better than any other father in the whole world! 🌑 God is our heavenly Father who hears our prayers.

Read Isaiah 65:24 aloud.

Ask: • **What does this verse tell us about God?**

• **How do you feel knowing God hears us before we even finish talking?**

• **Is there anyone else who knows exactly what you're going to ask before you even ask it?**

Say: It's an honor to be able to call God our Father and to know that he hears us when we pray!

SCENIC ROUTE

Bring in props to represent each of the people in authority, such as a paper crown for the king, a necktie for the president, a schoolbook for the principal, a hat for the police officer, a gavel for the judge, a piece of athletic equipment for the coach, and a Bible for God.

TOUR GUIDE TIP

If children don't know how to address people of authority, suggest titles such as Your Honor, Mister or Madam President, Sir, Ma'am, and so on.

TOUR GUIDE TIP

Not all of the children may be familiar with the different people named in this activity. Give kids a brief description of each job or position as you introduce the volunteers.

Items to Pack: paper, Bible, crayons or markers

STORY EXCURSION

(15 minutes)
Father to All

This activity allows children to reflect on a story about God's care.

Have a volunteer read Psalm 68:5 aloud to the class.

Say: **There are many people who don't have fathers here on earth to take care of them. Maybe their fathers have died, maybe their parents have divorced and the fathers have gone away. For whatever reason, not everyone has a father. This verse says that God is a father to those who don't have one. We're going to hear a true story about someone who looked to God as her father, and see what happened. As you listen to the story, draw a picture that shows either a part of the story or how you feel about what God did in this story.**

Distribute paper and crayons or markers, then read the story on page 24 to the class. Pause occasionally as you read to give kids time to reflect on what they're hearing and illustrate this as they like.

After the story, let children share their pictures and what they represent.

Ask: • **What do you think it was like for Gladys and all those children to rely on God instead of a father here on earth?**

• **How does Psalm 68:5 fit in with our story?**

• **Have you ever thought of trusting God to take care of you like a father would?**

• **How is God our father? How is God different from the fathers we know here on earth?**

FUN FACT

Here's how to say "father" in a few other languages:

Danish: *Fader*
Italian: *Padre* or *Babbo*
Dutch: *Pater* or *Papa*
French: *Pere*

Say: Gladys knew that 🌀 **God is our heavenly Father who hears our prayers. She was able to turn to God in a time of trouble and know that he would hear her.**

ADVENTURES IN GROWING

(10 minutes)
The Perfect Father

Have the kids form groups of three or four. Give each group a pen or pencil and paper.

Say: **When people want to hire someone to do a job for them, they usually write a few sentences telling what the job is and what the person who is hired will do. This is called a job description. What if you were going to write a job description for your dad? What would the perfect dad be like? Work with your group to make a job description for the perfect father.**

Items to Pack: paper and pens or pencils, Bible

The Story of Gladys Aylward

Gladys Aylward was born in London in the early 1900s and grew up wanting to be a missionary. She wanted to go to China and tell people there about God. But no group of missionaries would let her go with them. Gladys kept praying and working as a maid and saving her money, hoping that someday she would be able to go to China. God heard Gladys' prayers.

One day Gladys heard that a missionary in China needed help. The missionary was an older woman who ran an inn where people who were traveling into the mountains could stop and rest and eat. While the people were there, she would tell them about God. Gladys used the money she had saved to go to China and become a helper to the woman. A few months after Gladys arrived, the missionary died. Gladys would have to work as a missionary alone.

God took care of Gladys in amazing ways, and she began to take orphans—children without parents—into her home. A war broke out, and more and more children came to Gladys. Soon she had one hundred children in her care! And because of the bombing and the dangers of war, they all needed to escape!

Gladys began to pray, asking God what she should do. God heard her prayer. God knew the dangers facing Gladys and the one hundred children who didn't have fathers to take care of them. God used words from the Bible to encourage Gladys to escape to the mountains. So the next day Gladys and the children began walking. They had to walk over one hundred miles, and it took them many, many days, but God protected them and they all made it to safety.

Give the kids three minutes to create their descriptions, then gather the kids together. Have groups take turns reading their job descriptions until all the ideas have been shared.

Ask: • **Do you think anyone could actually be like the father you described? Why or why not?**

• **Which of the things you listed describe God?**

• **How is God our Father?**

• **Why does having God as our heavenly Father make it easier for us to pray to him?**

Read Matthew 6:25-26 aloud.

Ask: • What kinds of things do you worry about?

• Can your dad take care of these things? Can any dad? Why or why not?

• Do you think God can take care of them? Why or why not?

Say: God is the perfect Father. He not only cares about us, but he has the power to *take* care of us. 🌑 God is our heavenly Father who hears our prayers. Many times, he is already answering our prayers before we even pray them. When we pray, we can remember how much God loves us, and how much power he has to take care of us.

(5 minutes)
God Our Father

Read Jeremiah 29:11-12 aloud.

Say: God our heavenly Father has plans for us and listens to us.

Ask: • What are your plans for the future?

• Do you think God cares what we choose to do?

• How can we know his plans for us?

Lead the kids in the following rhyme, teaching them the hand motions to go along with it.

God our Father up above (point up)

Your plans for us are filled with love. (Cross arms over heart.)

You give us hope every day (hold hands out, palms up)

And always listen when we pray. (Fold hands in prayer.)

▲ TOUR GUIDE TIP Print the poem on newsprint so the children can learn it more quickly. Say it at least three times for those who don't read so that they can learn it also.

SOUVENIRS → (10 minutes)
Happy Father's Day!

Children will create cards to share their thoughts with God, their heavenly Father.

Say: Whether or not we have fathers here on earth, 🌑 God is our heavenly Father who hears our prayers. Let's make Father's Day cards for God and use these as written prayers to God.

Give each child a copy of the "Happy Father's Day" handout, and make the other supplies available. Have children complete the statements on the cards with words or pictures. Let kids personalize the open spaces with pictures or phrases they think God will like.

When children complete their cards, have them place these in their Travel Journals.

Items to Pack: "Happy Father's Day" handouts (p. 27), markers or crayons, pens or pencils. You may also wish to make glue, scissors, and assorted craft items available.

SCENIC ROUTE → If weather and your location permit, take children outside to collect small items to decorate their cards, such as leaves, wildflowers, or twigs.

FUN FACT

Father's Day was started in 1910 by Sonora Louise Smart Dodd, who wanted to honor her father, William Jackson Smart. The holiday was only celebrated in Spokane, Washington (Dodd's hometown), for many years. It is celebrated today in both the United States and Canada.

HOME AGAIN PRAYER

(5 minutes)

Perfect Father Prayer

Have children look at their descriptions of the perfect father again. Ask each child to silently choose a word or phrase that describes God. It's OK if children choose the same words. Explain that you will begin the prayer, and when you pause, children can call out these words. After all the children have had a turn calling out words that describe God as our perfect heavenly Father, you will finish the prayer.

Pray: **Our Father in heaven, thank you for listening to us when we pray. Thank you for taking care of us and answering our prayers. You are the perfect Father! You are** [have children call out words and phrases here].

We love you. Amen.

Happy Father's Day!   **Happy Father's Day!**   Happy Father's Day!

Father God, you're a good Father.
This is something great you've done:

Thank you, Father, for loving me.
Here's another thing I'm thankful for:

I need help. Father, please help me
with this:

"This, then,
is how you
should pray:
'Our Father in
heaven...' "
(MATTHEW 6:9a).

Hallowed Be Your Name
(Matthew 6:9b)

Pathway Point: 🌐 We can worship God through prayer.

In-Focus Verse: "...hallowed be your name" (Matthew 6:9b).

Travel Itinerary

How many times have we heard someone use the name of our Lord in a negative way? How would we feel if our own name were used in this manner? Most certainly we'd be offended. The Bible tells us that the name of the Lord is holy, set apart, worthy of the highest praise. When we speak God's name, we should do so with honor.

Children may not understand the words *hallowed* and *holy*, but most do understand what respect is, and this concept can help in teaching children about holiness. Through this lesson, you can help kids better understand the holiness of the Lord's name and how we can worship him.

DEPARTURE PRAYER (up to 5 minutes)

Say: Today we're going to learn how special God's name is and how 🌐 we can worship God through prayer. If a king or someone we really wanted to honor was coming through here, we would bow to show honor to that person. Let's bow before God to show him honor today.

Kneel with the children, then pray:

Dear Lord, we praise and worship your name because you are holy. We love you and honor you. Amen.

1st STOP DISCOVERY (15 minutes)
What's in a Name?

This activity allows children to explore the meanings of names.

Preparation: Write each of the following names of God on one side of an index card, and the meaning on the opposite side: Christ (Messiah and Anointed One), Immanuel (God With Us), El-Shaddai (God Almighty), El-Roi (God Who Sees Me), and Yahweh-Rohi (The Lord Is My Shepherd).

Give each child a blank index card. Have each child clearly print his or her first name on one side of the card. Then have children share the name books

TOUR GUIDE TIP The activities in this book have been designed for multi-age groups. Select from the activities, or adapt them as needed for your class.

Items to Pack: baby names books (check these out from your local library), index cards, pens or pencils, Bible

you've brought to look up their names and write the meaning on the opposite side. Help younger children as necessary.

Gather the cards, and read the meanings of the names aloud. See if children can guess which meaning goes with which name.

Ask: • **Does the meaning of your name tell who you are?**

• **Do you know how your parents chose your name?**

• **What name might describe you better?**

Say: Some parents choose names because they like the sound of the name, or because they want to name their child after someone special like a relative or person from the Bible, and some parents choose names because of their meanings. In Bible times the meanings of names were very important. In fact, God has several names. This time I'll read the name and see if you can think of the meaning.

Read the names on the cards you prepared and let children guess the meanings before you read the meanings from the other side.

Ask: • **Why do you think God has different names?**

• **Can you think of any other names of God from the Bible? If so, what are they?**

• **What do we learn about God from his names?**

Open your Bible to Matthew 6:9.

Say: **The Bible tells us other names for God. And as we learn about the Lord's Prayer, we learn something else about God's name. Last week we learned that God is our heavenly Father. The Lord's Prayer begins "Our Father in heaven" and continues "hallowed be your name." The word *hallowed* means "holy."**

Ask: • **What do you think "holy" means?**

• **Can you give any examples of something that is holy?**

• **What does it mean to say that God's name is holy?**

Say: *Holy* has a couple of meanings. First, it means "set apart." This is a way of saying God's name is very special and we should treat it with respect. *Holy* also means "perfect," or "pure." God is so perfect and pure that we are amazed at how holy he is! Because God is holy, we can worship him and give him honor and respect. Today we're learning that ● we can worship God through prayer.

FUN FACT The five most popular baby girl names in 2001 were Emily, Hannah, Madison, Samantha, and Ashley. The top five baby boy names were Jacob, Michael, Joshua, Matthew, and Andrew.

TOUR GUIDE TIP If you only have a couple of baby names books, have children begin this activity as they come into the class. This will spread out the use of the books over a longer period of time.

FUN FACT These famous people didn't like the names their parents gave them and changed them…

Thomas Cruise Mapother changed to Tom Cruise.

Norma Jean Mortensen Baker became Marilyn Monroe.

Margaret Mary Emily Anne Hyra is now Meg Ryan.

Eldrick Woods is better known as Tiger Woods.

Items to Pack: Bible, paper, markers or crayons, tape

TOUR GUIDE TIP

You can adapt this activity according to the number of children in your class. For smaller groups, have only one child illustrate each phrase, or join two phrases together. For larger classes, have three or more children illustrate each phrase.

TOUR GUIDE TIP

If you're able to leave the pictures up for several weeks, let them be a visual reminder of worshipping God through prayer. If you need to remove them immediately, let the children place their artwork in their Travel Journals.

STORY EXCURSION (15 minutes)

Psalms of Worship

Children will create a mural to represent a prayer of David.

Say: **The Bible tells us about a man named David. I'm going to share a few things about David to give you an idea of what he was like. As I'm telling you about David, I'll pause every now and then so you can make the sound effects. When I hold up my hand like this** (wave your hand in the air) **that means it's time for the sound effects to stop so I can keep telling the story. Here we go!**

David was the youngest in his family. He had a lot of older brothers who got to do the important jobs around their home. It was David's job to take care of the sheep (pause). **Sometimes this was dangerous work, because of the lions** (pause) **and bears** (pause) **that tried to attack the sheep** (pause) **and eat them. David was so brave that he would chase down the lion** (pause) **or bear** (pause), **rescue the sheep** (pause), **and kill the animal!**

Sometimes taking care of sheep (pause) **was quiet work. On these days David was able to relax. He would play his harp** (pause). **He would write songs to God and sing them** (pause). **Some of his songs were prayers to God asking for help. Some were prayers telling others how great God is. Others were prayers of worship, telling God how wonderful and holy he is. We can read a lot of these prayers in the Bible, in the book of Psalms.**

Give each child a piece of paper, and place the crayons or markers where the children can share them. Explain that you're going to read one of the prayers of David, and the kids can illustrate this prayer. Before they begin, read Psalm 100 aloud, with everyone listening. Then read it again slowly, and point to one or two children as you read each phrase. That will indicate that they are to illustrate this phrase in any way they like. For example, the first two children will illustrate "Shout for joy to the Lord, all the earth," the next two children will illustrate "Worship the Lord with gladness," and so on.

Allow time for children to draw their pictures. If you like, read the psalm aloud again several times as they work, to help them consider this prayer and call to worship.

When children have completed their drawings, read Psalm 100 aloud again, pausing after each phrase. When you pause, have the child or children who illustrated this phrase tape their pictures to the wall. Continue with the next phrase, and have the next group post their illustrations next to the first. Continue until you have read through the psalm and all the pictures are posted in their correct order.

Ask: • How did David worship God?

• Which of these things do you do as you pray to God?

• What words or phrases in this psalm remind us that God is holy or that he should be honored?

• What can we learn from David's example?

ADVENTURES
IN
GROWING

(15 minutes)
Make a Joyful Noise

Children will write prayers of worship.

Items to Pack: paper, pens or pencils

Have children form groups of four or five. Encourage older children to partner with younger ones.

Say: **Let's practice worshipping God through prayer. A prayer of worship, like Psalm 100, should tell God how great he is, just as a cheer for your favorite sports team would. A prayer of worship is not a prayer where we list all the things we need. It's a way of telling God we think he's the best!**

Explain that each group will write a prayer of worship and then share it with one or more other groups. Encourage kids to be creative. Suggest that they consider setting their prayer to music (they might use a popular tune and write new words to it), creating a rap or cheer, or writing a prayer they would all whisper together. Remind children that they can use some of the names of God in their prayers too.

After several minutes, have each group partner with another group, and let them share their prayers. Remind kids that even though they're letting others hear their prayer, they're really speaking to God.

After each group has shared its prayer of worship, gather kids together.

SCENIC ROUTE → Make a video of the kids sharing their prayers, and show it to them on the last week that you study the Lord's Prayer as a reminder of what they've learned.

Ask: • **How do you think God feels when he hears these prayers?**

• **How do you feel expressing these thoughts to God?**

• **Could you offer as much praise and worship to God if he wasn't holy? Why or why not?**

Say: **The prayers of David and the prayers you all have shared remind us that** ◓ **we can worship God through prayer.**

TOUR GUIDE TIP If your class is large, have groups partner with one or two other groups to share their prayers as time allows. If your class is smaller, have each group share its prayer with everyone.

(5 minutes)
Praise the Lord

Children will express words of worship from a psalm.

Say: **Let's read another of David's prayers of worship, in Psalm 148. In this psalm David repeats the phrase "praise the Lord" many times. Every time I point to you, I want all of you to stand, lift your hands high in the air, and shout, "Praise the Lord!" I'll read the other parts of the psalm.**

Practice pointing to the kids and having them do their part one or two times, then begin. Point to the kids every time you come to the phrase "praise the Lord," and let them participate in this prayer of praise to God.

Ask: • **How does this prayer help us to worship God?**

• **What are other words and actions that show we worship God?**

 (10 minutes)
Worship Your Name

Children will illustrate names of God and write words of praise to him.

Items to Pack: "Worship Your Name" handouts (p. 34), markers or crayons

As you pass out the handouts, say: **As we learn the Lord's Prayer, we learn that God is our Father and that God's name is holy. Let's say what we know of the Lord's Prayer so far.**

Lead the children in saying Matthew 6:9. If children don't know it yet, have them use their handouts for reference.

Say: **God's name is holy, just as God is holy. And because God is so perfect and awesome, ◔ we can worship God through prayer.**

At the top of the handouts, have each child write his or her name and the meaning of the name that the child learned earlier. Then have children read the names of God and draw a symbol or small picture to illustrate this name. If you have time, children can look up the verses where the names are used.

Have the children form pairs or trios. Have them answer these questions in their groups.

Ask: • **When you pray, what name do you use to refer to God?**

• **What's a different name for God that you'd like to use?**

• **How should we use the name of God? How should we not use God's name?**

• **How can these pictures or symbols help you remember to worship God when you pray?**

Have children place their handouts in their Travel Journals.

SCENIC ROUTE Let children join with partners and share prayers and praises. Encourage kids to update their Prayer Journals.

(5 minutes)

A Name Worthy of Praise

Have all the children stand in a circle and hold hands or link elbows.

Say: **We've learned that God is holy and that** **we can worship God when we pray. Let's worship God now by using some of God's names we've learned.**

Explain that you will pray, and when you pause, you'll squeeze the hand (or elbow) of the child on your right. This child will then call out one of God's names and squeeze the hand or elbow of the next child, and so on until everyone has had a turn. Then you will complete the prayer.

Pray: **Our Father in heaven, hallowed be your name. We praise you and worship you because you are holy. Your names tell us how special you are and how much we should honor you. You are** (pause for children to respond). **Your name is worthy of all our praise. Help us to remember to always keep your name holy. Amen.**

Worship Your Name

My name:

The meaning of my name:

A few names of God:

Prince of Peace
(Isaiah 9:6)

King of Glory
(Psalm 24:7)

Shepherd of Israel
(Psalm 80:1)

"Our Father in heaven, hallowed be your name"
(Matthew 6:9).

JOURNEY 5

Your Kingdom Come
(Matthew 6:10a)

Pathway Point: We can be a part of God's kingdom.

In-Focus Verse: "...your kingdom come" (Matthew 6:10a).

Travel Itinerary

During Jesus' day, the Roman Empire was the most powerful kingdom on earth. Rome's arm stretched from Persia to Egypt to Europe. Since the fall of Jerusalem in 587 B.C., the once-proud nation of Israel was reduced to being the occupied territories of the Babylonian, Macedonian, and now the Roman Empire. Israel had not experienced national sovereignty in nearly six hundred years. The nation awaited the promised Messiah who would establish the kingdom of God. When Jesus taught the disciples to pray "your kingdom come," he was tapping into a national longing for God to establish his order and bring liberation. Many in Jesus' day expected the Messiah to be a military ruler and use brute force to establish order. How could they have predicted how Jesus would establish his kingdom?

Today's kids can also misunderstand what God's kingdom is and how they can join it. There is a natural phase in a child's moral development in which they are very aware of issues of right and wrong. Many children assume that if they behave and go to church, they're automatically a part of God's kingdom. However, kids need to learn that they can't behave their way into God's kingdom. Entrance is by invitation only. It's God's gracious gift.

TOUR GUIDE TIP The activities in this book have been designed for multi-age groups. Select from the activities, or adapt them as needed for your class.

DEPARTURE PRAYER

(up to 5 minutes)

Preparation: Before class, place the candy inside the security box, and lock the box with the padlock.

Gather the children in a circle.

Say: **I've placed a yummy treat inside the box. You can have it if you unlock the lock.**

Allow the children to attempt to figure out the combination on their own. After a few minutes of letting the children struggle with the combination, ask:

• **Would you like me to give you the combination?**

Tell the children the combination, and allow one of them to open the box and pass out the treat. As children enjoy their treat, say: **You wanted to get into the box so you could have your treat. But you needed my help getting in. Today**

Items to Pack: combination padlock, security box, individually wrapped candy

Items to Pack: crayons, copies of "Come to Our Party" handout on page 42, scissors

we're going to learn that  we can be a part of God's kingdom. But we need God's help. Let's ask God to teach us how we can join his kingdom.

Gather the children in a circle.

Pray: **Dear God, today we want to learn how to be a part of your kingdom. Please help us to learn how we can be a part of your kingdom. We love you very much. Amen.**

1st STOP DISCOVERY (10 minutes)
Getting Ready for a Party
Children will create party invitations.

Say: **We're learning about the Lord's Prayer. Jesus told his friends to pray, "Our Father in heaven, hallowed be your name, your kingdom come." The "your kingdom come" part is what we'll be learning about today. In Jesus' day, everyone was waiting for a time when God would rule like a king. Everyone knew that God would be a great king, and everyone would be happy to be a part of his kingdom. What some people didn't know is that Jesus could help everyone join God's kingdom. We're going to learn more about God's kingdom today.**

Let's pretend that we are getting ready to have an amazing party for our friends. Let's make invitations to tell them about our party.

Give each child a copy of the handout and a pair of scissors. Place the crayons where children can reach them. Children will not need to write anything on these. Let them color the invitation then cut it out along the solid lines and fold it on the dotted lines.

Ask: • **What does it feel like when you get ready for a party?**

• **How do you choose who you will invite?**

• **How would you feel if the people you invited didn't come? Why?**

Say: **Jesus said that being a part of God's kingdom was like a rich man who invited people to come to his party. Let's see what happened. Maybe we can find out how we can be a part of God's kingdom.**

Set aside the invitations to be used later in the lesson.

STORY EXCURSION (5 minutes)
Sick and Lame

Children will prepare for the Bible story.

Items to Pack: Bible

Open your Bible to Luke 14.

Say: **In our Bible in Luke 14, Jesus told a story. In the story there was a group of people that were sick and lame, or unable to walk. Let's pretend that we're those sick and lame people. I'll read a statement. If what I say applies to you, then pretend that you have whatever ailment I read. If more than one thing applies to you, then pretend that *each* thing is wrong with you.**

Read the following sentences. Pause between each one so the children can decide if it applies to them and how they will play-act their illness.

• If you didn't spend time with God this week in prayer or reading the Bible, pretend that your left leg doesn't work.

• If you said something unkind to anyone this week, then pretend that you are blind.

• If you disobeyed your mom or dad this week, then pretend that your right leg doesn't work.

Ask: • **What would it be like to really be sick or lame?**

• **How you do think other people would treat you? Why?**

Say: **If you're now one of the sick and lame, I want you to keep pretending to be sick all throughout our Bible story. If you're not one of the sick and the lame, you're going to pretend to be the rich man's friends.**

TOUR GUIDE TIP If you have a handicapped child in your class, call the family ahead of time and tell them about your lesson. Ask if the child would feel comfortable talking about the handicap and how people treat him or her. By forewarning the family and inviting the child to help you teach, you can diffuse any sensitive emotions and involve the child in a special way.

(15 minutes)
Come to the Party

Children will re-enact the Bible story.

Items to Pack: toy phone, "Party Time" script

Have the sick and lame people stay in character and move to one side of the room. Have the rich man's friends sit on the other side of the room.

Say: **We're ready to tell our Bible story. I need your help. If you're one of the sick or lame people, I want you to shout, "I'd love to come!" any time you hear me say the word "party." If you're one of the rich man's friends and you hear me say the word "party," reply, "I'm too busy!"**

Practice this one time with the children.

Say: **I'm going to pretend to be the rich man. Ready?**

Have the toy telephone handy, and read the "Party Time" script on page 40. When you are finished reading the script, ask:

Items to Pack: Bible

Items to Pack: The invitations the children made in 1st Stop Discovery, pens, glue sticks, and copies of "God's Invitation" handout on page 43 on brightly colored paper

• How is joining the kingdom of God like the rich man's party?

• Why do you think the rich people decided not to come to the party? How do you think this made the rich man feel?

• How do you think the sick and the lame people felt when they were invited to the party?

• What does this story tell us about how to get into God's kingdom?

Say: ◐ We can be a part of God's kingdom. God wants everyone to be a part of his kingdom. He's like the rich man who invited everyone to his party. God has invited us to be a part of his kingdom. But we must say "yes" to his invitation.

ADVENTURES IN GROWING

(15 minutes)
Getting Into the Kingdom

Children will consider what it takes to get into the kingdom of heaven.

Say: I'm going to introduce you to three people. Each one has an idea of how he or she can get into God's kingdom. Once you hear each story, we'll decide if that person understands what it takes to get into the kingdom of heaven.

Read each of the introductions found on the "Getting In" box on page 41. After each introduction, ask the following questions:

• How does this person think that he or she can get into God's kingdom?

• Will this way work? Why or why not?

After you've read all the introductions, ask a volunteer to read Ephesians 2:8-9.

Ask: • What could you tell these people, and those who think like them, about being a part of God's kingdom?

Say: ◐ We can be a part of God's kingdom. But we can't do any work to get in. God wants us to do good things like going to church and being kind. However, these things will not get us into God's kingdom. The only way to be a part of God's kingdom is to say "yes" to God's invitation.

SOUVENIRS →

(10 minutes)
Price of the Party

Children will consider the cost Jesus paid for us to enter his kingdom.

Say: It's fun to throw a party, but it costs a lot of money.

Ask: • What kind of things do people buy to get ready for a party?

• How much do parties cost?

• If parties cost money, why do parents throw birthday parties for their children?

• What do you think it cost God to invite us to his party?

Say: **God loves us, and he wants us to be a part of his kingdom party. But all the bad things that we do, like the things that made us "sick and lame" in the Bible story, keep us from being near God. So God sent Jesus to die on a cross to take away all the bad things we do. That's what it cost God so** we **can be a part of God's kingdom.**

Have children open up the invitations they made earlier and look at the shape of this cutout. Explain that this shape is a reminder of the price Jesus paid for us to be a part of God's kingdom. Jesus paid this price because he loves us.

Have children glue their opened invitations onto the indicated space on the handout. Then let them complete this souvenir with the directions on the paper. Help younger students who cannot read. When children have finished, they may add these to their Travel Journals.

Say: **When Jesus died on the cross, he paid the price so we could be invited into God's kingdom. Anybody who believes that Jesus did this and says "yes" to God's invitation to come to the party can be a part of God's kingdom.**

<table>
<tr><td>

HOME AGAIN PRAYER

</td><td>

(up to 10 minutes)
In God's Kingdom

</td></tr>
</table>

Gather the children around you in a circle. Give each child about a teaspoon of confetti. Ask children to hold this in their hands until you explain how it will be used.

Say: **As Jesus taught us how to pray, he included the phrase "your kingdom come."** We **can be a part of God's kingdom. God has invited everyone to be a part of his kingdom. All we have to do is say "yes." Let's praise God for letting us be a part of his kingdom.**

Explain that you will begin a prayer, and after you finish, each child will take a turn praying in the same manner. First, everyone will say the portion of the Lord's Prayer that you've learned so far. Then you'll say, "Dear God, the best part of being in your kingdom is…" and you'll finish the sentence. After you finish, you'll throw your confetti into the center of the circle as an expression of celebration and praise. Then the next person in the circle will finish the sentence as he or she desires and throw confetti. Continue until each child has had a turn, then all say "Amen!" together.

Pray: **Our Father in heaven, hallowed be your name, your kingdom come. Dear God, the best part of being in your kingdom is…"**

Amen!

Items to Pack: confetti

TOUR GUIDE TIP Your janitor will be thankful if you take the time to find the vacuum cleaner and clean up the confetti after your lesson.

Party Time

Rich Man: Well that does it! I'm all ready for my **party**. *(Pause.)* I've been planning it for weeks. I have all of the food ready. My servants have all gone out and given invitations to all my friends. I hope they come to my **party.** *(Pause.)* I'll just wait by the telephone for their replies.

There's a call now! *(Pick up the telephone.)* Hello, you're calling about my **party**? *(Pause.)* You don't have time to come? You've bought some land and you want to go look at it? Well, OK. I *am* disappointed. Goodbye. *(Hang up the phone.)*

Can you believe it? My friend Joe is too busy for my **party**! *(Pause.)* Doesn't he know how important this **party** is? *(Pause.)* Or how long I've worked to get my **party** ready? *(Pause.)*

Oh, another phone call. *(Pick up the telephone.)* Hello Samantha…you just bought a pair of oxen to work in your field. That's great. But you are coming to my…no? You're too busy to come to my **party**? *(Pause.)* But you've known that I've been working on this **party** for months, right? *(Pause.)* I've spared no cost; it's going to be a great **party**. *(Pause.)* I see. *(Hang up the telephone.)*

(Deflated) This is frustrating. None of the people who call themselves my friends are coming. Oh wait, another telephone call. *(Hurriedly pick up the telephone.)* Yeah, James. You just got married? Fantastic! Hey, did you get my invitation? You did? Do you think you'll come to my **party**? *(Pause.)* No. You're too busy. Of course you are. OK…goodbye.

Not one of my so-called friends is coming to my **party**! *(Pause.)* I've prepared so much food. My house is decorated. By golly, I *am* having a **party**! *(Pause.)* If my friends won't come, I'll invite other people.

(Pick up the phone.) Tell my servants that I want them to invite all of the sick and the lame people to come to my **party**! *(Pause.)* Yes, I'm serious. Tell them they are invited to the most amazing **party** *(pause)* they'll ever experience. *(Hang up the phone.)*

I want to make people happy. I want to be friends with them. I hope the sick and the lame people will accept my invitation.

There's the phone again. *(Pick up the phone.)* Hello? All of the sick and the poor will come? Fantastic! There is still more room? Well then, go out into the city and invite *anyone* who wants to come to my **party** to come. *(Pause.)* Anyone who will accept my invitation is welcome. Everyone is welcome to come to my **party**! *(Pause.)*

Getting In

Introduction 1

My name is Charles Church. My family goes to church all the time. I've haven't missed a day of church in a year. My family goes three hours a week—two hours on Sunday and one on Wednesday. I've gotten prizes for my attendance and for always bringing my Bible. The way I see it, I go to church so much that God *has* to be impressed. He'll see my attendance award and let me into his kingdom.

Introduction 2

My name is Dora Do-Good. I do lots of good things. Last year I saved fifty dollars of my allowance money and gave it to a food drive for poor people. I volunteer to read to younger students at school every week. I always volunteer to do extra chores around the house. Nobody does more good things than me! I think this is the kind of stuff that makes God *want* me to be a part of his kingdom. If I'm not in God's kingdom, then who is?

Introduction 3

I'm Easy Eddie. Am I in God's kingdom? Sure I am. I mean, who isn't? If God is love, then how could anyone *not* be a part of God's kingdom? God's isn't going to tell people they can't be a part of his kingdom because they don't believe the right things or because they did some small thing wrong. Everyone is going to be a part of God's party whether they've heard of Jesus or not!

Come to our party!

God's Invitation

"Our Father in heaven, hallowed be your name, your kingdom come"
(Matthew 6:9b-10a).

Jesus paid the cost so I can be a part of God's kingdom. Here's what I want to say to Jesus:

_____

_____

_____

_____

Here are the names of two friends I can invite to join God's kingdom:

_____

_____

_____

JOURNEY 6

Your Will Be Done on Earth As It Is in Heaven (Matthew 6:10b)

Pathway Point: God's desires and plans should guide our prayers.

In-Focus Verse: "...your will be done on earth as it is in heaven" (Matthew 6:10b).

Travel Itinerary

Sometimes prayer gets treated as if it's a spiritual form of catalog shopping. "Dear Lord, I need this, and this, and this." There is nothing wrong with asking God to provide us with our needs and even wants. However, God isn't just our gracious provider; God is our king. The prior phrase of the Lord's Prayer, "your kingdom come" acknowledges this fact, and by acknowledging God as king, we also acknowledge that he has a will, a strategy for running his kingdom, and rules that govern how his citizenry should live. This week's phrase, "your will be done on earth as it is in heaven," demonstrates a heartfelt desire that everything that happens on this earth submit to God's rule the same way that all of heaven does.

Kids can learn that it is not enough to call Jesus "Lord" or "king." We need to teach children how to be God's obedient citizens. One of the most powerful practices that an adult or child can do in prayer is to pray for things that he or she knows are God's will. God promises to respond to these prayers and answer them in a mighty way. When kids pray for help in being loving, or for help in telling their friends about Jesus, they *will* see God's hand.

> **TOUR GUIDE TIP**
>
> The activities in this book have been designed for multi-age groups. Select from the activities, or adapt them as needed for your class.

Items to Pack: yellow construction paper, tape, scissors

DEPARTURE PRAYER

(up to 10 minutes)

Preparation: Before class make a crown from the construction paper and tape.

Gather the children in a circle. Have the children take turns wearing the crown and saying what laws they would make if they were king. When every child has had a chance to be "king," ask:

• **Why did you choose to make those laws?**

• **God is a king. What kinds of laws does God give us to obey?**

• **Why do you think God gives us these laws?**

Say: God is King. He gives us good laws so we'll be happy. When we obey God, we treat each other with love. When Jesus taught his friends to pray, he told them to pray, "Your will be done on earth as it is in heaven." Jesus wanted us to pray that everyone would obey God on earth the same way that the angels obey God in heaven. Let's pray.

Pray: Dear God, we know you are our king. Teach us to pray for things that help your desires and plans to happen. Amen.

1st STOP DISCOVERY (10 minutes)
Remote Controlled

Children will be guided by others to a treat.

Items to Pack: clean, soft blindfolds; a plate of treats

Say: Let's play a game called "Remote Controlled." I'm going to have you get into pairs to try to find a plate of treats. One of you gets to see. You are the guide. Your partner has to wear a blindfold. If you are blindfolded, you can ask your guide questions like "Should I go forward?" or "Should I turn around?" The guide can only reply with "yes" or "no" answers.

Have the children pair off, and give each pair a blindfold. Once all the blindfolds are on, set out the plate of treats. Let the children find their way to the treats according to the rules you've given them. As each pair arrives at the plate, let the child who was blindfolded have a treat. Once all the pairs have arrived at the plate, have the partners switch roles and play again so that those who were guides in the first round will also get a treat.

As the children are enjoying their treats, ask:

• When you were blindfolded, was it easy or hard to follow the instructions of your guide? Why?

• How was listening to your guide like praying to God?

• How was listening to your guide different from praying to God?

Say: Today we are going to learn that ⬤ God's desires and plans should guide our prayers. Your guide wanted you to find the treat. When you asked your guide for help, you got it. God wants us to obey him here on earth, the same way the angels obey him in heaven. When we ask God to help us obey him, he will answer our prayers.

SCENIC ROUTE →

Bring in a remote-controlled car, and let the children play with it. Discuss how the car was designed to do what the controller tells it to do. When we pray, we should be asking God for help doing the things we know that God wants us to do.

FUN FACT

Did you know that the Lewis and Clark Expedition was guided by an American Indian woman named Sacagawea? She helped Lewis and Clark communicate with the native Americans they met on the way. She carried her infant son on her back throughout most of the journey. She was such an important guide that her face is on the U.S. one-dollar coin.

Items to Pack: sheet of red poster board, packing tape, paint stick, marker, paper, tape, overhead projector, thermal transparency page, blanket, table, Bible

STORY EXCURSION

(20 minutes)
Finding Direction

Children will re-enact a portion of Paul's journeys.

Preparation: Before class, copy the "Macedonian Vision" page (p. 51) onto a transparency page. Make a stop sign from the red poster board, and tape the paint stick to it as a handle. Write the words "Asia," "Bithynia," "Troas," and "Macedonia" on four sheets of paper. Tape one sheet of paper on each wall. Place the overhead projector on the floor, pointed toward the wall marked "Macedonia" with the transparency of the Macedonian man ready to project. Place the table near the "Troas" wall, and drape the blanket over it to make a tent.

Gather the children on the floor, outside of the tent, and open your Bible to Acts 16.

Say: **Our Bible story is found in Acts 16. Paul and his friends were on a great journey to tell everyone they met about what we learned last week—that we can be part of God's kingdom. Paul and his friends knew that this was God's will because Jesus told his friends to tell everyone they met about him. The leaders of the church had prayed about how to obey this command. They decided that Paul and his friends should tell people from other countries about Jesus. Paul and his friends went out to obey Jesus' desires and plans. They just weren't sure where to go next.** Show the children the wall marked "Asia."

Paul and his friends decided to go to Asia to tell people about Jesus. Let's go to Asia. Have the children walk to the wall marked "Asia." When they almost get to the wall, stand in front of them and hold up the stop sign. **The Holy Spirit told them to stop. They were not supposed to go to Asia to tell about Jesus.**

Have children find partners and sit down with their partners to discuss the following questions. After allowing time for discussion, have one or two pairs share their answers before moving on to the next question.

Ask: • **How do you think that Paul and his friends felt when the Holy Spirit told them not to go to Asia?**

• **Why do you think the Holy Spirit told them "no"?**

• **What would you have done if you were Paul?**

Say: **Paul and his friends knew that it was still God's desire and plan that they tell others about Jesus. So they decided to go to Bithynia. Let's travel to Bithynia.** Have the children get up and walk to the wall marked "Bithynia." Just before they get to the wall, hold up the stop sign.

The Holy Spirit did not let them go to Bithynia, either. This was the

TOUR GUIDE TIP

Be certain that you're using a thermal (copier-friendly) transparency when copying the page. The high heat in the copy process will melt a regular transparency to the drum of your copier.

SCENIC ROUTE →

Set up a real tent instead of the table with a blanket over it. You might even include a few sleeping bags to get kids into the traveling and camping mood!

FUN FACT

The ancient Arabs used a tool called a kamal to help them navigate. They used the kamal to measure their position by the North Star. The word *kamal* means "guide."

second time that the Holy Spirit told them "no." Again have children find partners (different partners from before) and discuss the following questions.

Ask: • **How would you feel if you were Paul and the Holy Spirit said "no" to your plans twice?**

• **Have you ever had a hard time doing something that God wanted you to do? If so, tell about that time.**

Say: Paul and his friends didn't get discouraged. They knew that the Holy Spirit was guiding them as they tried to accomplish God's plans and desires. They traveled to Troas. Lead the children to the "Troas" wall. **This time the Holy Spirit did not tell them "no." Night fell and Paul's party went to sleep.**

Have the children crawl under the table tent and pretend to sleep. Turn out the lights to make it seem more like nighttime.

Say: **That night God appeared to Paul in a vision, or a dream.** Turn on the overhead projector and project the picture of the Macedonian man on the wall. "Wake" the children and show them the picture.

In Paul's vision he saw a man from Macedonia. The man begged Paul to come to Macedonia and help them. Paul and his friends immediately went to Macedonia. Have children get up and move to the "Macedonia" wall.

When they got there, they told everyone that they could find about Jesus!

Have children again form pairs and sit down to discuss these questions:

Ask: • **Why do you think God gave Paul the vision of the Macedonian man?**

• **How can God guide us when we want help obeying his plans and desires?**

• **What should you do when you want God's help in obeying his plans and will?**

Say: Paul accomplished God's plans and will because he paid attention when God was guiding him. God wants to guide us, too. There are things that we *know* that God wants us to do, like telling others about Jesus. When we pray and ask God to help us do these things, he will. ◕ **God's desires and plans should guide our prayers.**

(10 minutes)
Guided Prayers

Children will consider what they already know to be God's will.

Preparation: Tape sheets of newsprint to the walls where children can reach them.

Read 1 John 5:14-15 aloud.

Say: **This verse means that God promises to answer our prayers when we**

TOUR GUIDE TIP

Some children might not understand who the Holy Spirit is. Explain that the Holy Spirit is God, just like the Father and the Son. One of the things that the Holy Spirit does is guide us.

Items to Pack: newsprint, markers, tape, Bible

SCENIC ROUTE

Have the kids make a simple compass by stroking a needle over a magnet in the same direction at least fifty times. Place the needle on a small piece of cardboard in a shallow bowl of water. The needle will point north. Talk about how a compass points us in the right direction and how knowing the Bible can guide how we pray.

pray for things that are God's desires and plans. When we want what God wants, God answers our prayers. Let's make a list of things that we know that are in God's will.

Have the children brainstorm things that they know God wants, like "obeying our parents" or "being kind." Give the children five minutes to brainstorm and write their answers on the sheets of newsprint. Then have children sit where they can see the sheets of newsprint and consider them during this discussion.

Ask: • **How do you know whether something is God's desire or not?**

• **Why should God's desires and plans guide how we pray?**

• **How will knowing that God answers us, when we pray for things that he wants, change the way we pray?**

Say: We learn what God's desires and plans are when we read the Bible. When we pray to God to answer prayers about *his* plans, we know that God will answer. ◐ God's desires and plans should guide our prayers.

(10 minutes)
Kingdom Come
Children will create skits showing how the world would be if people obeyed God's will.

Say: This week's part of the Lord's Prayer is "your will be done on earth as it is in heaven." When we pray this, we're asking that people would obey God on earth the same way that angels obey him in heaven. Let's imagine what that would be like.

Have children form groups of about four or five. Explain that each group can pick one thing from the lists on the walls. They should do this without discussion between groups, and it's OK if more than one group chooses the same item. Tell kids that they have five minutes to create a short skit showing what it would be like if everyone obeyed this part of God's will.

After five minutes have each group present its skit.

Ask: • **How would it feel to live in a world where everybody followed God's desires and plans in this way?**

• **How can you obey God in this area this week?**

Say: Life on earth would be more like life in heaven if we would obey God's desires and plans. ◐ God's desires and plans should guide our prayers.

 **SOUVENIRS** (10 minutes)
Map-It!

Give each child a copy of the "Map-It" page.

Ask: • **How does a map guide us?**

• **How are God's desires and plans like a map for our prayers?**

• **Why should we pray that God's desires and plans happen?**

Say: **This map is your prayer map. I want you to think of three things you know are a part of God's plans and desires. I want you to write them in the three blanks on your map. For example, you might choose "being patient" or "inviting my friends to church."**

Allow time for children to write down their ideas. Then continue.

Say: **Have you ever seen pictures of an old map from an adventure movie? Have you noticed how they turn brown and stained? Let's make our maps look like they're old. This will remind us that praying for things that God desires and plans has *always* been a good idea.**

Show the children how to wet a teabag in the warm water and squeeze the excess water out of the bag. Demonstrate how to blot the tea bag on a map to make the map look fatigued. Allow the children to blot their maps until they look authentically weathered. Set them aside to dry. Use the paper towels to dry hands, wipe spills, and blot excess water from the maps.

Say: **When you pray in the coming weeks, pray for the three things you wrote on your map. Watch how God answers your prayers.**

HOME AGAIN PRAYER (5 minutes)
Pick a Prayer

Preparation: Before class choose candies of any four colors and place in a bowl. Make a chart similar to the following example that uses the colors available to you.

Items to Pack: copies of "Map-It!" from page 52, pens or pencils, teabags, a large bowl of warm water, paper towels

TOUR GUIDE TIP Be sure to use pencils or ballpoint pens for this activity. The ink in markers or felt pens will run when the paper gets wet.

TOUR GUIDE TIP The activity will work best with warm, but not hot, water.

Items to Pack: bowl of colorful candies such as M&M's or Skittles, chart as described below left

---

Pick-Up Prayers

Red: Pray for the courage to tell a friend about Jesus.

Blue: Pray that God will help you be kind—even to the people who aren't kind to you.

Green: Pray that God will help you remember to read your Bible every day this week.

Yellow: Pray that God will help you obey your parents.

Say: Let's practice 🌀 letting God's desires and plans guide our prayers. We are going to pass around the bowl. When it comes to you, close your eyes and pick out one piece of candy. Look at the chart to see what you should pray for. Everything on the chart is something that God wants for us. Pray aloud as the chart directs you, then pass the bowl. After you pray, you can eat the candy as a reminder of how good life "tastes" when God's plans happen.

Pass the bowl around the circle. Once everyone has had a chance to pray, close by praying: **Dear God, help us to want the things that you want. Help us to pray for things that matter to you. May your desires and plans happen on earth the same way that they do in heaven. Amen.**

Macedonian Vision

MAP-IT!

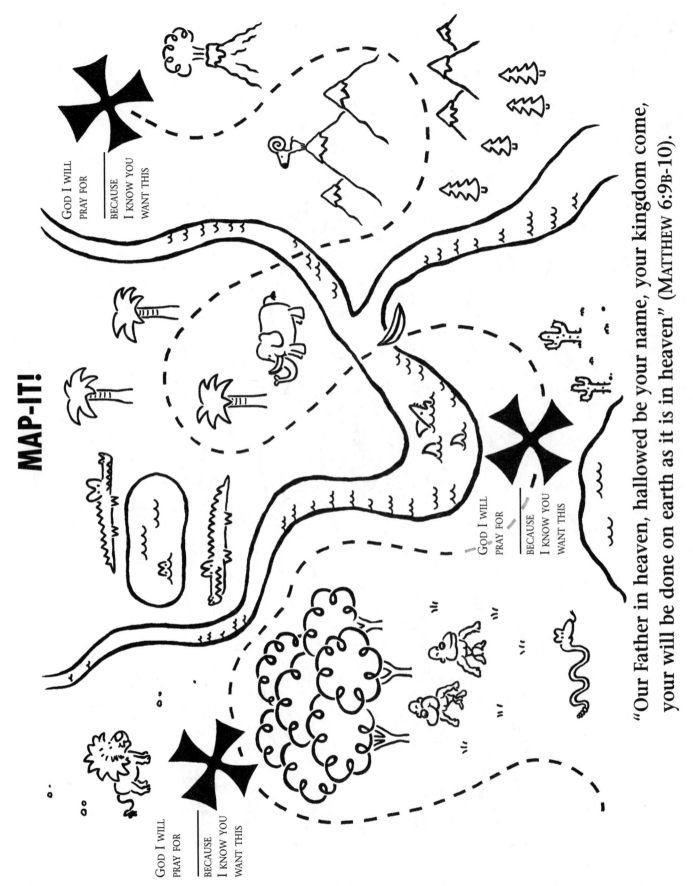

GOD I WILL
PRAY FOR _____
BECAUSE _____
I KNOW YOU
WANT THIS

GOD I WILL
PRAY FOR _____
BECAUSE _____
I KNOW YOU
WANT THIS

GOD I WILL
PRAY FOR _____
BECAUSE _____
I KNOW YOU
WANT THIS

"Our Father in heaven, hallowed be your name, your kingdom come, your will be done on earth as it is in heaven" (MATTHEW 6:9b-10).

JOURNEY 7

Give Us Today Our Daily Bread
(Matthew 6:11)

Pathway Point:  We can ask God to provide for our needs.

In-Focus Verse: "Give us today our daily bread" (Matthew 6:11).

Travel Itinerary

In the Lord's Prayer, Jesus taught the disciples to pray first for God's will and then for their own needs. Jesus teaches us how to put Matthew 6:33 into practice in our prayers as we "seek first his kingdom," then ask for the rest. The phrase, "daily bread" also reminded Jesus' listeners of the forty years in Israel's history when God daily provided manna. The people had grumbled and God responded graciously. Jesus instructs his followers not to approach God with a grumbling heart, but with humility.

Many children living in North America never experience true want because of the relative prosperity of this continent. Asking God to meet their needs might seem pointless to children living in prosperity. However, this prayer teaches children that God is their provider and they can turn to him with their needs. And there are truly many children around us in great need. This lesson gives these children hope in God's provision.

TOUR GUIDE TIP The activities in this book have been designed for multi-age groups. Select from the activities, or adapt them as needed for your class.

| DEPARTURE PRAYER | (5 minutes) |

Have children say with you the portion of the Lord's Prayer that you've learned so far: "Our Father in heaven, hallowed be your name, your kingdom come, your will be done on earth as it is in heaven."

Say: **Today we're learning the part of the Lord's Prayer that says "give us today our daily bread." Jesus was teaching his friends that**  **we can ask God to provide for our needs. Let's remind each other of this part of the prayer.**

Have children sit in a circle. Give each child a small bit of the slice of bread. After everyone has a piece of bread, pray: **Dear God, thank you for giving us everything that we need, including our daily bread. Thanks for taking care of us. It feels good to be loved. Amen.**

Let the children eat their bread.

Items to Pack: slice of bread

Items to Pack: old pots and pans or aluminum pie tins

TOUR GUIDE TIP

Your room is sure to be noisy for this activity. Consider a fun signal to reel in the kids if they get carried away with their banging and clanging. Tell the kids when they see you place your pot on your head, it's time to listen for the next situation. Practice a couple of times before you begin the activity.

SCENIC ROUTE →

Tape record the children pretending to complain about the situations. Play the tape back to them. Talk about what it's like to be around someone who complains a lot.

1ST STOP DISCOVERY (10 minutes)

Got the Gripes?

Children will loudly complain about things that don't go their way.

Pass out the pots and pans.

Say: **Let's find out what things turn us into complainers. I'm going to read a list of things that might make you want to complain. If what I read would make you complain a whole lot, bang your pot a lot. If you would complain a little bit, just make a little bit of noise. If you don't think you would complain at all, don't make any sounds with your pot.**

Read the following list, and pause between each item so the children have a chance to bang on their pots.

- **You find out you're having brussels sprouts for dinner.**
- **Your sister ate the last piece of cake.**
- **Your teacher gave you extra homework.**
- **Your brother is sick and your dad asked you to do his chores on top of your regular chores.**
- **Your mom signs you up for the football team.**
- **Your dad grounds you from video games for a week.**
- **A movie you really want to see is opening today. You stand in line for hours to get a ticket. The person in front of you gets the last ticket. You won't get to see the movie today.**
- **Your mom signs you up for ballet classes.**

Collect all the pots and pans, and set them aside.

Ask: • **How is complaining like the sound of the pots and pans?**

• **How do you feel when you're around a complainer?**

• **What should we do when things don't go our way or we need something that we don't have?**

Say: **Sometimes it's easy to complain when things aren't going our way. We can be upset when we can't have things that we want or need. In our Bible story today, we are going to meet some people who did a lot of complaining. But we're going to learn a better way. ◐ We can ask God to provide for our needs.**

54

(20 minutes)
Meals to Go

Children will re-enact the story of the Israelites in the wilderness.

Preparation: Lay out a tablecloth on the floor.

Have the children sit on the floor around the tablecloth. Open your Bible to Numbers 11.

Say: **Last week, we learned what Jesus meant when he said, "Your will be done on earth as it is in heaven." Can anyone tell me in their own words what this means?** Allow time for children to respond.

This week we're learning the next part of the Lord's Prayer which says, "Give us today our daily bread." When Jesus' friends heard this, it reminded them of a special time in their nation's history. Let's look at that special time. Our Bible story comes from two books in the Bible, Numbers 11 and Exodus 16–17:6. God's people had been slaves in Egypt. Moses led them out of Egypt. Before they left, they baked some bread to eat on the way.

Give each child a saltine cracker. Ask children to wait until you tell them to eat it.

Say: **God told them to leave in a hurry because the Egyptians would come after them. Let's pretend we're on the run.** Lead the children in running around the room. If your room is small, have children run in place. Have the children take their crackers with them. Return to your original spot, and say: **That was tiring! I'm hungry. Let's eat.** Have the children eat their saltines. **God's people had a long way to travel to get to the good place God wanted them to live. It's time to travel again. Let's go.** Lead the children in walking around the room.

Say: **It's been a long couple of days of traveling through the desert. Let's eat.** Let the children point out that they're out of crackers. Tell them that they have a problem because they still have a long, long journey ahead.

Ask: • **How do you think God's people felt when they realized that they were out of food?**

• **What would you do if you thought you might starve in the middle of a desert?**

Say: **The people began to grumble. Use your voices to tell me what you think the people's grumbling was like.** Wait for children to respond. **The people were so upset, they told Moses that they'd rather return to being slaves! They remembered all the food in Egypt and wished they still lived there, even if it meant they would be slaves again.**

SCENIC ROUTE → Add to the fun by playing Follow the Leader each time you "travel" to a new location on this journey.

FUN FACT Did you know the good food that God's people longed for was fish, cucumbers, melons, leeks, onions, and garlic? How would you like *that* for dinner?

SCENIC ROUTE → Have the children make paper airplanes to represent the quail. Have them throw them into the center of the circle. Talk about what it would be like to watch a flock of birds appear to be your food and what it would take to prepare them as a meal.

SCENIC ROUTE → Pass around a bowl with chunks of cooked chicken in it to let the kids have an idea of what the quail tasted like.

TOUR GUIDE TIP Be aware that some children in your class may be from families with true financial needs. God can provide for our needs, but there are Christians who are hungry or who suffer from lack of provisions. Challenge students to consider how God might use them to meet the needs of others in your church, community, or in the world. Children might pray for the needs of others, or take tangible action such as having a canned food drive, collecting coats or shoes in the winter, or bringing donations toward other needs.

God heard the people grumble. God was not happy about their complaining, but he loved them and knew that they needed food. God had Moses tell the people to go to sleep and when they woke up they would see that God could provide for their needs.

Have the children pretend to sleep on the floor. While their eyes are closed, place broken pieces of graham crackers all over the tablecloth. Have the children "wake up."

Say: **When the people woke up, the ground was covered with a special type of bread. The Israelites called the bread "manna." Manna means "what is it?"**

Let children pick up the graham cracker pieces and eat them.

Say: **The people were happy with their new food for a while. Then they began to be tired of eating the same food week in and week out. They began grumbling again. Let me hear what they probably sounded like.** Pause for children to complain.

Moses was upset. The people were complaining again. And Moses didn't have any food to give them. There were thousands and thousands of Israelites. How could he give them the meat that they wanted to eat?

Ask: • **If you were Moses, how would you feel?**

• **If you were Moses, what would you do?**

Say: **Moses prayed to God. He told God about the people's complaining. Moses asked God to provide for their needs. God sent a flock of quail to the camp. The people caught the quail, cooked them, and ate them.**

Ask: • **How do you think the people felt when they realized that God had provided for their needs?**

• **How does God provide for your needs?**

• **Why is it important to ask God to provide for the things we need?**

Say: **You would have thought that the people would have learned that they could ask God to provide for their needs. After all, God provided them with manna and quail. However, they didn't remember this lesson very long. Moses led them to a different part of the desert.**

"Travel" around the room again.

Say: **In this part of the desert, there wasn't any water. When the water that they brought with them ran out, they began to grumble. The people were so upset that Moses thought they might *kill* him.** Have the children loudly complain again.

Moses prayed to God to provide for their need for water. God told Moses to strike a large rock with his staff. What a strange thing for God to say! You

can't get water out of a rock! However, Moses trusted God to provide for his needs. So Moses did what God asked, and water poured out. Moses knew to ask God to provide for all of their needs! And God provided.

Ask: • How do you think God felt when the people grumbled for water even after he had provided them with manna and quail?

• How do you think God feels when you complain about things you don't have?

• Why should we ask God to provide for our needs?

Say: God loves to take care of our needs. God loves his people. The Israelites didn't need to complain. God wasn't about to let them starve. We don't need to be worried or complain to have our needs met. God promises to provide for our needs. All we have to do is ask! Jesus taught us to pray, "Give us today our daily bread."

SCENIC ROUTE →

Have the children make their own manna to take home. Have the children spread honey on bread. Place the bread in a toaster oven until crisp. Use a sharp knife to cut the bread into croutons for the children. Have the children take their "manna" croutons home in plastic sandwich bags.

ADVENTURES IN GROWING

(15 minutes)
Picture This

Children will evaluate what things they want and what things they need.

Set the magazines, catalogs, and scissors where children can reach them.

Say: Let's look through these magazines and catalogs to find pictures of things we can ask God for. If you find a picture of something, go ahead and cut it out.

Give the children five minutes to find their pictures, then collect the pictures. Have the children sit in a circle around you. Set the poster board in the middle of the circle. Use the marker to divide the poster board into two columns. Write the word "Wants" at the top of one column and the word "Needs" on the other.

Say: Bread is one of the most basic foods that we need. When Jesus taught us to pray "Give us today our daily bread," he was telling us to ask for the things that we need. God doesn't promise to give us everything that we want, but he will give us what we need. Let's go through our pictures and decide together whether these are things that we want or things that we need.

Hold up each picture and let the children decide if it is a picture of a want or a picture of a need. Let a volunteer apply glue to the back of the picture and place it on the correct side of the poster board. Repeat the process with every picture.

Items to Pack: old magazines or catalogs, scissors, glue stick, marker, large piece of poster board

TOUR GUIDE TIP

Be sure to go through the magazines beforehand to check for any pictures or articles that would be inappropriate for young eyes.

FUN FACT

Did you know that God took care of Israel's clothing needs too? It took Israel forty years to make it into the Promised Land. God miraculously kept their clothing and sandals from wearing out. See Deuteronomy 29:5 to check it out!

Ask: • What are other things you might put in the "need" column that we didn't have pictures of? in the "want" column?

• Why doesn't God always give us what we want?

• What's the best part of knowing that we can ask God for what we need?

Say: There's nothing wrong with asking God for things we want. But God knows what things would be good for us to have and what things we'd be better off without. God takes care of what we need. ● We can ask God to provide for our needs.

SOUVENIRS → (10 minutes)
Breakfast Flakes

Give each child a copy of the "New Every Morning" page. Set the glue and crayons on the table. Pass the bowl around the circle and let the children taste a piece of cereal. Say: **Manna might have looked a little bit like this cereal. The Bible says that manna looked like little scales or flakes. Manna tasted sweet like honey. Every morning, when we get up, we can get our daily bread by going to the cupboard and pouring ourselves a bowl of cereal. The Israelites got up early while the dew was still on the ground and picked up their daily bread—manna—off the ground.**

Ask: • What would it be like to wake up to manna on the ground every day?

• How does God meet your need for "daily bread"?

• Why does God want us to ask him to provide for all of our needs?

Say: ● **We can ask God to provide for our needs. We don't need to get worried or grumble. We have a great, loving God who wants to take care of us. Let's decorate these pictures to remind us that we can ask God to provide for all of our needs.**

Have the children color their pictures. Show them how to glue the frosted flakes to the ground areas of the picture to remind them of manna. Have kids fill in the blanks with a need and what they will say to God about that need. As they work, share about a time when things were tough and God provided for your needs. Kids need powerful examples of adults who know how to pray.

When children have finished their pages, have them place them in their Travel Journals.

(up to 5 minutes)
Pray-Dough

Have the children sit in a circle. Give each child a piece of modeling dough.

Say: **Mold your dough into something that you need God to provide. We'll ask God to provide us with our daily bread, which represents our greatest needs.**

Give the children two minutes to shape their dough. Explain that you'll pray aloud, and when you pause, children may silently pray for what is represented by their dough object.

Pray: **Dear God, we have many things that we need you to provide for us. Thanks so much for loving us and *wanting* to provide for our needs. We will ask you for everything that we need. Right now we ask you to provide** (pause for a minute for children to pray silently). **Give us today our daily bread. Amen.**

Allow the children to take their molded dough home as a reminder to ask God to provide for their needs.

Items to Pack: modeling dough

NEW EVERY MORNING

Here is one thing I need:

Here is what I will say to God about this need:

"Our Father in heaven, hallowed be your name, your kingdom come, your will be done on earth as it is in heaven. **Give us today our daily bread**" (MATTHEW 6:9B-11).

Forgive Us Our Debts
(Matthew 6:12a)

Pathway Point:  We can ask God for forgiveness.

In-Focus Verse: "Forgive us our debts" (Matthew 6:12a).

Travel Itinerary

Children have varied experiences with sin, largely determined by their up-bringing. For the vast majority of children, sin is more of a concept than something that relates to their own lives. For these children, moral language centers on the words "appropriate" or "inappropriate." The idea that they might act in a way that is offensive to a holy God is foreign to them. Children need to be aware that God is perfect and that when we do wrong things we do them *against* God. But we also need to teach children that God is forgiving. Through his Son Jesus, God is ready to forgive us whenever we pray. Jesus taught his disciples to pray for forgiveness because each of us sins, and we all need grace.

TOUR GUIDE TIP The activities in this book have been designed for multi-age groups. Select from the activities, or adapt them as needed for your class.

DEPARTURE PRAYER (5 minutes)

Have the children gather in a circle. Spread newspaper on the floor. Set the mirror on the newspaper. Squirt shaving cream all over the mirror so the children can't see their reflections.

Ask: • **How useful is this mirror right now?**

Say: Today we're going to learn that  **we can ask God for forgiveness. When God forgives us, he cleans us. Let's ask God to help us learn why this is important. "Dear God, please teach us why it is important to ask you for forgiveness. Amen."** Squirt the mirror with the water. Pass the squirt bottle around the circle and give each child a chance to clean some of the shaving cream off the mirror.

Pray: **God, we're glad we can ask you for forgiveness. Thank you for forgiving us and making us clean. Please show us today why it's so important to turn to you whenever we do wrong things. Amen.**

Items to Pack: mirror, shaving cream, spray bottle with water, newspaper

1st STOP DISCOVERY (10 minutes)
Fashion Faux Pas

In this activity, children will avoid one person covered with symbols of sin.

Preparation: Before class, write the Ten Commandments as paraphrased in the box on page 62 on a large piece of newsprint.

Items to Pack: self-stick notes, vinyl raincoat, pencils, newsprint, marker, Bible

THE TEN COMMANDMENTS

1. You shall have no other gods before me.

2. You shall not make any idols.

3. Speak God's name with respect.

4. Set aside a special day for God.

5. Honor your father and mother.

6. You shall not kill.

7. Be true to your husband or wife.

8. You shall not steal.

9. You shall not lie.

10. You shall not want what others have.

TOUR GUIDE TIP

If you don't have access to a raincoat, you can make a vest from a paper grocery bag or a plastic trash bag. Cut out a hole for the head and the arms. Don't substitute with fabric clothing, because the sticky notes will not stick to fabric.

Gather the children around you. Show the children the poster board with the Ten Commandments.

Say: **God gave us ten good rules that he wants us to follow. Sometimes we don't obey them. I want you to silently think of times you have not kept these rules. For example, when you read "You shall not lie," you might think of a time that you cheated at a board game.**

Without asking for specific examples, ask children to think of which of these rules that they've broken. Have children write the numbers of the rules they've broken on sticky notes. For example, if a child has broken rule number 10, he or she would simply write "10" on a sticky note as a representation of that sin.

Ask: • **Do you think it's a big deal if we disobey one of God's rules? Why or why not?**

• **What do you do when you disobey God?**

• **What do you think God does when we break these rules?**

Say: **When we break one of God's rules, it's called sin. Even if it seems like a tiny thing to us, it's a big deal to God. Let's find out what the Bible says about how God reacts when we sin.** Read Habakkuk 1:13a aloud. **This verse says that God can't even look at evil or sin. Let's play a game to help us understand this.**

Have one child wear the raincoat. Have the other children place their sticky notes all over the raincoat.

Say: **Stand up and talk with those around you about the best thing that happened in your week. You can talk to whoever you want, but whatever you do, don't look at the sticky notes. Pretend they hurt your eyes!**

Give the group a few minutes to talk while the child wearing the raincoat moves around. After a couple of minutes, have a different child wear the raincoat. Give others a chance to wear the raincoat as time allows. Then have the children return to their seats, and ask the child now wearing the raincoat to stand beside you.

Ask: • **What was it like to wear the raincoat?**

• **What was it like to have to avoid looking at the raincoat?**

• **How does this game help you understand the fact that God can't look at sin or be near it?**

Say: **God is perfect. He can't be near sin. When we sin, it messes up our friendship with God, just like it was hard to talk to the person with the raincoat. But ☻ we can ask God for forgiveness.** Remove one or two of the sticky notes from the raincoat. **When we ask God to forgive us, God will take away** the bad things we do so we can be friends with him, just like I can take the sins off this raincoat. Let's find out more about what the Bible says about God's forgiveness.

STORY EXCURSION (15 minutes)
Courtroom Drama

Children will participate in a courtroom scene based on Zechariah 3.

Say: **We're adding to what we know of the Lord's Prayer. Let's review what we've learned so far.**

Have the children say with you the portion of the Lord's Prayer that you've learned in the previous weeks. "Our Father in heaven, hallowed be your name, your kingdom come, your will be done on earth as it is in heaven. Give us today our daily bread."

Say: **As Jesus taught his friends to pray, the next thing he taught was for us to pray, "Forgive us our debts." This means that when we do something wrong there is a price to pay. But ⬤ we can ask God to forgive us so we don't have to get the punishment we deserve. Today's Bible adventure will help us understand this verse.**

Place a table and chair at the head of the classroom to be the judge's bench.

Say: **Today's Bible adventure comes from the book of Zechariah, chapter 3. Zechariah was a prophet. A prophet was someone God gave special messages to. God gave Zechariah a special dream called a vision. In the vision, Zechariah saw a courtroom scene something like this one.**

Pick one child to play the part of Satan and another to play the part of the Judge. Pick one child to play the part of Joshua the high priest. Give each of these children a script. You will read the part of the Angel of God and help other children participate as indicated in the script. Have "Joshua" wear the raincoat covered with sticky notes. Tell the rest of the children that they will be the Jury. It's their job to decide if Joshua is guilty or not.

Present the drama for your class, then ask the following questions.

Ask: **• How do you think Joshua the high priest felt when God forgave him?**

• How do you feel when you've sinned? How do you think God feels about it?

• Who do we hurt when we sin?

• What should you do when you've sinned?

Say: **Joshua the high priest knew that he had sinned against God. He**

Items to Pack: gavel (or small hammer), raincoat and notes from the "Fashion Faux Pas" activity, 3 copies of "Order in the Court" (p. 66), table and chair, large white shirt, ball cap

SCENIC ROUTE → Make your courtroom come to life. Borrow a black graduation gown for the Judge to wear.

FUN FACT Only God can clean our hearts, but there are computer-controlled vacuum cleaners to tidy your floors without any help from you. Now if there was only a robot to fold the laundry...

TOUR GUIDE TIP Many children are familiar with the other Joshua in the Bible—the one who led Israel into the Promised Land. Explain that this is a different Joshua. This Joshua was the high priest, and he stood before God as a representative of God's people.

63

knew that there was nothing that he could do to make his sins go away. However, God surprised him and forgave his sins. God wants to forgive us of our sins. All we have to do is 🌑 pray and ask God for forgiveness. God will forgive us.

ADVENTURES IN GROWING

(15 minutes)
Mint Condition

Give each child a few tarnished pennies.

Say: **When these pennies were first made, they were perfect. There was nothing wrong with them. They were bright, shiny copper pennies. But over the years, they started to tarnish. They don't look nice anymore. They're dull and dirty.**

Ask: • **How is this like what sin does to us?**

• **Why should we care that sin changes us?**

Say: **I want you to clean off the pennies. Make them nice and shiny again. Take a baby wipe, and rub your pennies until they look brand-new.**

Give each child a baby wipe. Let the children rub their pennies for several minutes. If they get discouraged, prompt them to keep going. Say things like, "Maybe you just need to try longer." After a few minutes,

Ask: • **How is this like our ability to get rid of our sins by ourselves?**

• **What does sin do to our friendship with God?**

• **What should we do when we sin?**

Give each child a plastic cup. Pour one-half inch of vinegar into each cup. Have children fill their plastic spoons with baking soda and stir it into the vinegar. Have them drop their pennies into the mixture. While the mixture is working, read 1 John 1:9 aloud.

Say: **This verse means that when we confess, or admit, our sins to God, he will forgive us and make us clean again. All we have to do is ask.**

Have the children remove their pennies from the solution.

Ask: • **How is the vinegar and baking soda like God's power to forgive?**

• **Why can we trust God to forgive us?**

Say: 🌑 **We can ask God for forgiveness whenever we do something wrong. We don't have the power to get rid of the wrong things we do—just like we couldn't clean our own pennies. But God forgives us and makes us clean, every time we ask him to! The part of the Lord's Prayer that says "Forgive us our debts" reminds us to go straight to God when we do wrong things. God loves us and wants to forgive us. Awesome!**

SOUVENIRS → Clean Again

Children will create "new clothes" to represent God's forgiveness.

Pass out a copy of "Clean Again" to each child. Set out the ink stamps on the table.

Say: **I want you to think of things that you've done in the past that you know are wrong. Place your thumb in the inkpad, and then stamp your thumbprint on the boy's clothing each time you think of something you've done wrong.** Give the children time to do this.

Ask: • **How are these pictures like what happens when we sin?**

• **How can we become clean again when we've sinned?**

Say: **When we pray, God promises to forgive us. In Zechariah's vision, the Angel of God gave Joshua a new, clean robe. Let's give the boy in our picture a new robe.**

Show the children how to cut out the pattern at the bottom of the page and use it to trace the outline of a robe on a piece of white felt. Have the children cut out the robe and glue it over the boy's dirty clothes.

Ask: • **What's the best thing about knowing that God forgives us when we pray?**

Say: 🕐 **We can ask God for forgiveness when we do something wrong. God promises to take away our dirty sins and make us clean again. We don't need to be afraid of talking to God when we sin. God wants to forgive us.**

Have children add these pages to their Travel Journals.

SCENIC ROUTE →

Purchase some disappearing ink. Spill it on your clothes, then pretend to be upset because ink doesn't come out. When the ink disappears, talk about how when we pray and ask God for forgiveness, he makes our sins disappear.

HOME AGAIN PRAYER

(10 minutes)
Crossed Out

Children will place their "sins" on a cross.

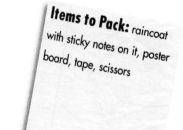

Preparation: Before class cut out the shape of a cross from the poster board. Fasten the cross to the wall with tape.

Say: **The Bible says that we all do things that we know are wrong. We've already thought about ways we've broken God's rules, and we've learned that 🕐 we can ask God to forgive us for doing these things. The reason God can forgive us is because Jesus paid the price, the debt, for our sins when he died on the cross.**

Have each child take a sticky note that represents a sin from the raincoat and place it on the cross.

Say: **When we pray for forgiveness, what Jesus did on the cross takes away our sins.**

Pray: **Dear God, all of us have sinned and we want to be forgiven. Thank you for forgiving us. Jesus, thank you for dying on the cross and taking away our sins. We love you very much. Amen.**

"ORDER IN THE COURT"

Judge: *(Pounds gavel)* Hear ye, hear ye. Now hearing the case of "Joshua the High Priest versus God." All rise. *(Wait for everyone to stand up.)* I am the honorable Judge Justice. You may all be seated. What are the charges?

Satan: I say that Joshua the high priest is guilty. Guilty, guilty, guilty. Throw the book at him, your honor! It's obvious that he's a sinner!

Judge: *(Pounds the gavel)* Order in my courtroom! Satan, I know you're an accuser, but you will behave in my court. What is it that Joshua has done? How do you know he's guilty?

Satan: *(Points to Joshua's coat)* Look at the sin all over him! He's covered with it!

Judge: Hmmm. This is a serious charge. I can see that this robe is dirty with sin. Joshua, did you bring your own lawyer?

(Joshua shakes head "no.")

Judge: Is there anything you can say in your defense?

(Joshua shakes head "no.")

Judge: Jury, is Joshua guilty or not?

(Give the Jury a few minutes to vote before continuing.)

Judge: The Jury has decided you are _____ *(say what the Jury decided)*. But no matter what they think, I get to make the final decision, and I say you are guilty. You have gone against God's rules.

Satan: I win! I win! I love finding people guilty! Guilty, guilty, guilty!

Angel of God: Not so fast, Satan. I am the Angel of God and I'm here to say that God has forgiven Joshua. Joshua is like a burning stick that God has pulled from the fire before it could be burned up. Take off his filthy clothes.

(Have two children take the raincoat off Joshua.)

Angel of God: Now, put these clean clothes on Joshua.

(Have two children help Joshua put on the clean shirt and the hat.)

Angel of God: Joshua, God has forgiven you. God has taken away your sins and given you clean clothes. You will obey God and do the important things God has for you to do.

Satan: Wait! He's guilty! This isn't fair!

Judge: You're right. Joshua doesn't deserve to be forgiven, but God is more powerful than I am, and God has forgiven Joshua. I declare Joshua innocent. Joshua, you are a free man! Court is adjourned!

(Have all the children cheer.)

Clean Again

"Our Father in heaven, hallowed be your name, your kingdom come, your will be done on earth as it is in heaven. Give us today our daily bread. **Forgive us our debts**" (MATTHEW 6:9B-12A).

Permission to photocopy this handout from *Kids' Travel Guide to the Lord's Prayer* granted for local church use.
Copyright © Group Publishing, Inc., P.O. Box 481, Loveland, CO 80539. www.grouppublishing.com

As We Also Have Forgiven Our Debtors (Matthew 6:12b)

Pathway Point: 🌐 God asks us to forgive others.

In-Focus Verse: "As we also have forgiven our debtors" (Matthew 6:12b).

Travel Itinerary

Forgiveness goes against our natural instincts. It's something we all have to be taught to do. As you observe your class, you notice some children ignore conflicts, others abandon relationships when conflict arises, and others try to prove themselves right even at the expense of others. A better solution is to practice forgiveness, which doesn't deny or ignore wrong done by both parties, nor does it abandon the relationship. Instead, one who forgives reaches out to heal the rift caused by conflict.

The world says our motivation in forgiving should be to free ourselves from the destructive effects of holding grudges. But the Bible encourages us to forgive as a response to the unmerited forgiveness we have received. As Christians, we understand our own humble position before God. We are sinners who need God's forgiveness daily. When we understand how generously we have been forgiven, we are enabled to forgive others from the heart.

DEPARTURE PRAYER

(5 minutes)

Gather children into a circle. Review what you've learned so far of the Lord's Prayer by having children say with you, "Our Father in heaven, hallowed be your name, your kingdom come, your will be done on earth as it is in heaven. Give us today our daily bread. Forgive us our debts."

Show the magazine picture before the Departure Prayer. Explain that as you pray, you'll pass the picture around. Children should silently make a tear in the picture and pass it on.

Pray: **Dear God, when others hurt us, it's difficult to forgive them. Often we don't even *want* to forgive. We need your help. Even though we've done things that displease you, you still love and forgive us. Help us understand how much you have loved and forgiven us so we will want to forgive others, too. Amen.**

Show kids the torn picture, and say: **The people in this picture are nearly torn apart! This reminds me of what happens when we don't forgive each**

TOUR GUIDE TIP The activities in this book have been designed for multi-age groups. Select from the activities, or adapt them as needed for your class.

TOUR GUIDE TIP Review with kids the meaning of "debts" and "debtors." If your church uses different words in praying this petition of the Lord's Prayer, clarify this for kids. Whether the words used are "debts," "trespasses," or "sins," our prayer is the same. By no longer holding others' sins against them, we show we truly believe God has completely forgiven us.

Items to Pack: full-page magazine picture of two or more people

TOUR GUIDE TIP If you have more than fifteen students in your class, have children form two or more circles for this prayer activity.

other. Our friendships get torn apart. Last week we learned that Jesus taught his disciples, and us, to ask God to forgive our sins. The Lord's Prayer says, "Forgive us our debts," and then continues, "as we also have forgiven our debtors." Learning to forgive is part of God's plan to help us mend our broken friendships.

STOP Loads of Trouble

(10 minutes)

In this activity, kids will imagine what it's like to be weighed down by unforgiveness.

Items to Pack: newsprint, marker, tape

Preparation: Before children arrive, make two signs with the newsprint. On one write "No way!" and tape this to one wall. On the second sheet write "I will forgive" and tape this to the opposite wall.

Say: **Forgiving others can be hard. Sometimes people really disappoint us or hurt us. Let's see how hard or easy each of you think it is to forgive others.**

Show kids the two signs. Explain that you're going to read several statements. Kids should move toward the "I will forgive" sign if they think they'd be able to forgive in the specific situation. They should move to the "No way!" sign if there's no way they would forgive in that situation. Kids may stand in various spots in the middle if they're not sure or might consider forgiving.

Read these statements, pausing after each one to let kids move about the room to demonstrate their ability to forgive in that situation:

• **Your teacher gave you lots of homework on the weekend. You had other plans, but had to cancel them because of your teacher.**

• **Your little brother left his toys out and Mom made you pick them up.**

• **Your sister borrowed your favorite jacket and spilled juice on it.**

• **Your friend got to be team captain at recess and didn't choose you for his or her team.**

• **You asked for the last piece of dessert but someone else ate it.**

• **Your brother borrowed your video game and lost it.**

• **You called your friend, left a message, and your friend never called you back.**

• **Your parents made you help clean out the garage when you wanted to go to a friend's house.**

Have kids return to their seats and form groups of three or four. Have children discuss the following questions in their groups. After about two minutes of discussion, have one or two groups report to the entire group before you move on to the next question.

TOUR GUIDE TIP

You may have a child in your class who mentions an abusive situation as being difficult to forgive. Talk with this child privately, and then notify the proper authorities according to your church's policy and state laws. Follow up to be sure the child receives help. Clarify that forgiving someone does not mean that the sin of the abuser is acceptable or can continue unchecked.

Ask: • What situations are the easiest to forgive and why?

• Which are the most difficult for you to forgive? Why?

• What other things have happened to you that are even more difficult to forgive?

• Is there anything that you would never be willing to forgive someone for doing? If so, what is the situation and why wouldn't you forgive?

• How do you feel when it is hard to forgive others?

Say: 🌑 God asks us to forgive others even when it's hard or when they don't deserve it. God forgives us no matter what we do, and wants us to offer that same forgiveness to others. Let's look at a story Jesus told in the Bible to help us understand the importance of forgiveness even more.

STORY EXCURSION (15 minutes)
Deep in Debt

Kids will participate in a retelling of the parable of the unmerciful servant.

Items to Pack: Bible, index cards, pen, blue marker, red marker

Preparation: Before class, write the names of super-expensive items on half of the index cards, such as a jet plane, a diamond necklace, or a mansion. If possible, name a different item on each of the cards. Write "Joe" on the back of each of these cards. Write the name of one very inexpensive item on each of the remaining cards, such as a pencil, a rubber band, a toothbrush, and so on. Write "Bob" on the back of each of these cards. Make enough cards so that each child will have one.

Read Matthew 18:21-35 aloud.

Say: Jesus told this story to show how important it is that we forgive others. Let's retell the story using things that people own today to help us understand even more clearly what Jesus was saying.

Distribute the cards to the class and explain that you're going to have everyone participate in a drama. Each person with a "Joe" card will need to partner with someone with a "Bob" card. If you have an uneven number of students, have one child partner with you. Explain that those with the "Joe" cards will do the actions you read for Joe. Those with the "Bob" cards will do the actions you read for Bob.

Say: The Rich Ruler was looking through the royal books one day and discovered that one of his employees, Joe, had borrowed quite a lot from him. So the Rich Ruler called Joe in and said, "Hey Joe! Time to pay back all you borrowed. What exactly did you borrow from me anyway? Stand up and tell me."

TOUR GUIDE TIP Instead of writing "Joe" or "Bob" on the index cards, use cards of two different colors, and adapt the activity accordingly.

Have all the Joes stand and call out the items they borrowed.

Say: "Well I hope you enjoyed what you borrowed," said the Rich Ruler. "Now it's time to repay the loan."

Joe shook his head sadly. He had used up all the money and wouldn't be able to pay it back. The Rich Ruler said, "If you can't pay back the money, I'll have to sell your family and everything that you have. It's the only way to get my money back."

Joe fell to his knees and began begging the Rich Ruler for mercy. "Please be patient!" Joe said. "I'll work hard and pay you back. Please don't sell my family!"

The Rich Ruler thought for a moment, then decided he would forgive the debt Joe owed him. "You don't have to repay me after all, and I won't sell your family. I forgive the debt that you owe. You can tear up the paper that tells what you borrowed, to show that I forgive that debt." So Joe tore up the paper, jumped up and down with joy, and started home to celebrate.

But just as Joe was leaving the Rich Ruler's office, he bumped into Bob. Bob borrowed a tiny thing from Joe. What was it?

Have all the Bobs stand and call out what they borrowed.

Say: Joe was incredibly angry that Bob had not repaid him. "Pay me right now or I'll hurt you!" he demanded. Bob shook with fear, fell to his knees, and begged, "Please be patient with me, Joe! I'll pay you back soon!"

But Joe refused. He shook his fist and demanded that Bob be thrown into prison until he could pay off the tiny debt. When the Rich Ruler heard about this, he called Joe back to his office.

"I canceled your huge debt because you begged for mercy," the Rich Ruler said. "Shouldn't you have had mercy on Bob just like I had mercy on you?" Then the Rich Ruler turned Joe over to the jailers to be tortured until he could pay for the expensive item he'd borrowed.

Have children put all the cards and pieces of cards into the trash, then gather them for discussion.

Ask: • How is the story we acted out like the story that Jesus told in the Bible?

• How would you feel if you owed a huge debt, then found out you didn't have to pay?

• What huge debt do we owe to God? How did Jesus pay this debt?

• How can we show Jesus we're thankful that he paid the price of punishment for our sins?

FUN FACT

How often *does* God forgive us? Suppose we sin one time per hour. Sin isn't just wrong actions others can see, but also selfish attitudes and hurtful thoughts no one but God knows about. Multiply that one sin per hour by sixteen waking hours a day, then by seven days a week, and then by fifty-two weeks in a year. By the time we're ten years old, we've already needed God's forgiveness at least 58,240 times! Aren't you glad God is so generous with his forgiveness?

FUN FACT

In the parable of the unmerciful servant, we're told the servant owed the king ten thousand talents while his fellow servant owed a hundred denarii. How do those two debts compare? In present-day value, the servant owed the king millions of dollars, whereas his fellow servant owed him what could be earned in three or four months of work!

• If Jesus forgave us the huge debt of sin that we could never pay ourselves, how should we treat others who sin against us? Can you do this? Why or why not?

• What does the Bible say will happen to those who don't forgive others?

Say: Just one tiny sin is enough to keep us away from God, and we've all sinned a lot! Think how big our debt of sin must be! Jesus died on the cross and took the punishment for our sins so that we can know God. Because God forgives us, ◐ God asks us to forgive others.

ADVENTURES IN GROWING

(10 minutes)
Comic Relief

Children will visually erase comic scenarios, then compare this to forgiveness.

Open your Bible and read Jeremiah 31:34b and Ephesians 4:32.

Say: These verses remind us that when God forgives us, he no longer remembers the wrong things we've done. ◐ God asks us to forgive others just as he forgives us.

Give each child a piece of Silly Putty modeling clay, and demonstrate how to transfer a picture by pressing the Silly Putty over the comic strip. Show children how they can stretch the putty to create different facial expressions on the comic strip characters. Let kids create angry or mad faces from the comic strip characters with the putty. Then have them squeeze the Silly Putty into a ball to erase the picture. Give kids a few minutes to transfer and erase several pictures.

Ask: • Suppose you transferred a picture and never erased it. How is that like when we don't forgive someone?

• How is erasing pictures like God forgiving us?

• How do you feel knowing that God doesn't remember your sins?

• How do you feel knowing that God expects you to forgive others just as he's forgiven you?

Say: When we don't forgive someone, it is as if we have a picture of that person's sin in our heads. We keep looking at it over and over. ◐ God asks us to forgive others and put those pictures out of our minds.

TOUR GUIDE TIP

Collect comic pages for several days. Cut comic strips apart so kids can work in pairs or trios. One "egg" of Silly Putty holds enough for two children.

FUN FACT

Silly Putty was discovered during World War II by researchers trying to make artificial rubber. It was first marketed to the public in 1950. More than three hundred million eggs of Silly Putty have been sold. That's more than 4,500 tons!

SCENIC ROUTE →

Make your own putty by mixing ½ cup white glue with ¼ cup liquid starch. For best results, add the liquid starch 1 tablespoon at a time, mixing thoroughly before adding more starch.

SCENIC ROUTE →

Go outside and give kids sidewalk chalk to make their drawings. When everyone has finished, together say, "Forgive as the Lord forgave you. Colossians 3:13." Then use a garden hose with a spray attachment to wash away the pictures.

TOUR GUIDE TIP

If a dry-erase board or chalkboard is not available for your group, spread a white plastic tablecloth on the floor, and allow children to draw with washable markers. Provide kids with spray misters and paper towels to erase their drawings.

(15 minutes)
Clean Slate

Children will erase things to remind them of the importance of forgiveness.

Write "Forgive as the Lord forgave you. Colossians 3:13b" across the top of the dry-erase board or chalkboard, and read it aloud.

Provide each child with a dry-erase marker or chalk.

Say: **Let's draw pictures that will help us think about how God forgives us and about how** 🌑 **God asks us to forgive others.**

Have each child use a small section of the board to write a word or draw a picture of something for which they need God's forgiveness. If they don't feel comfortable with letting others see what they've done wrong, they can create a symbol to represent the sin or simply write the word "sin." When children are finished, say: **Let's pray and ask God to forgive us for what we've done wrong.**

Pray: **Dear God, thank you for loving us enough to send Jesus to die on the cross and take the punishment for our sins. Please forgive us for all the wrong things we've done.**

Let one or two of the children erase all the drawings to represent God's forgiveness. If you have enough erasers, let each child erase his or her own picture. Then tell kids to write a word or draw a picture of something for which they can forgive someone else. Encourage kids to be specific about things others have done to them. When everyone is finished, gather the group to pray again.

Pray: **Dear God, because you've forgiven us, we know that we can forgive others. Help us to offer the same forgiveness to others that you've offered to us. Amen.**

Tell kids to completely erase all the words and pictures.

Ask: • **How does it feel to look at the board after it is cleaned?**

• **Erasing the board is easy. Why is it sometimes hard to forgive?**

• **What can make forgiving easier?**

Say: **When we remember that God has forgiven us for so much, we become more willing to extend that same forgiveness to others when they sin against us.**

SOUVENIRS (10 minutes)
Forgiven Friends

Kids will "mend" a friendship while learning how to ask for forgiveness and forgive others.

Items to Pack: copy of "Forgiven Friends" (p. 76) for each child, 2 adhesive bandages per child, crayons or markers, ballpoint pens

Say: **Find a partner, and talk about things we say or do that can hurt friendships. As you talk, tear the picture of the two friends down the middle, separating them.**

Allow a few minutes for children to do this.

Say: **Write words on the adhesive bandages that would help two friends forgive each other, for example, "I'm sorry" or "I forgive you." Use the bandages to stick the two friends back together and mend the friendship.**

Provide supplies for the children to finish their pages.

Say: **When we let God's love and forgiveness show in our lives, it helps us to grow closer to God and to others.**

Let children color their pages as time allows.

Remind kids to put their "Forgiven Friends" pages in their Travel Journals.

HOME AGAIN PRAYER (5 minutes)
Penny Prayers

Items to Pack: two pennies, stack of play money held together with a rubber band

Hold a stack of play money in one hand and two pennies in the other hand. Gather children in a circle. As you begin to pray, pass the stack of play money around the circle.

Pray: **Dear God, we know you forgive us so often. You forgive the wrong things we do. You forgive the wrong things we say. You forgive our selfish, hurtful thoughts. You're always happy to forgive us and promise not to remember our sins. Thank you for forgiving us so freely.** (Begin passing the pennies.) **Lord, the sins of others against us are tiny compared to the sins you forgive us for doing. Help us remember ⬤ you ask us to forgive others. When it is hard to forgive, help us. Let us feel so thankful about being forgiven by you that we're happy to forgive others. In Jesus' name, amen.**

Forgiven Friends

GOD ASKS US TO FORGIVE OTHERS.

"Our Father in heaven, hallowed be your name, your kingdom come, your will be done on earth as it is in heaven. Give us today our daily bread. Forgive us our debts **as we also have forgiven our debtors**" (MATTHEW 6:9B-12).

And Lead Us Not Into Temptation
(Matthew 6:13a)

Pathway Point: God can give us strength.

In-Focus Verse: "And lead us not into temptation" (Matthew 6:13a).

Travel Itinerary

When children are young, morality is primarily based on fear of punishment. As they get older, kids can learn to choose right behaviors as a response to God's love. Although they may still be tempted to give in to selfish desires, they may rely on God to help them avoid wrong and choose what's right.

Peer relationships among children also exert an increasing influence over the choices kids make. Having friends who participate in dangerous or sinful activities can increase the attractiveness of these behaviors to children. Safeguard your kids by reminding them that God is actively involved in helping them conquer temptation.

TOUR GUIDE TIP The activities in this book have been designed for multi-age groups. Select from the activities, or adapt them as needed for your class.

DEPARTURE PRAYER (5 minutes)

Say: **When the disciples asked Jesus to teach them to pray, he taught them the Lord's Prayer. This prayer helps us, too, by serving as an example of the things we can talk about with God. Let's review what we've learned of the Lord's Prayer so far.**

Have children say what they've learned of the Lord's Prayer. "Our Father in heaven, hallowed be your name, your kingdom come, your will be done on earth as it is in heaven. Give us today our daily bread. Forgive us our debts, as we also have forgiven our debtors."

Say: **Today we'll learn the next part of the Lord's Prayer: "And lead us not into temptation."**

Have kids form a large circle, holding hands or linking elbows. Direct kids to take slow, small steps toward the center of the circle as you pray so that by the end of the prayer, kids are standing shoulder to shoulder.

Say: **As we pray and move toward the center of the circle, think about how prayer pulls us closer to God.**

Pray: **Dear God, every day we make choices. Sometimes we choose the right thing, but other times, doing wrong seems easier or more fun. Temptations crowd around us, leading us away from your path. Keep us close to you and give us strength to choose what is right. Amen.**

TOUR GUIDE TIP

Use any kind of party noisemakers for this activity, such as horns, whistles, or rattles. Or pull out hand-held rhythm instruments such as jingle bells, maracas, or finger cymbals.

FUN FACT

Cookies are a temptation for just about everyone! Did you know that Oreo cookies are the best-selling cookies in the United States, and over 362 billion Oreos have been sold? That's a lot of temptation!

 **(15 minutes)**
Noise or Not

Kids will determine how good they are at resisting temptation.

Have children stand in a circle.

Say: **I'm going to hand out noisemakers, but I don't want you to make any sounds with them. Even if you're tempted, hold your noisemaker so that it will not make a sound. If you can't resist the temptation to make a sound with your instrument, we'll know right away because we'll hear it. If you can't resist the temptation and make a noise, I'll silently point to you and that means you'll have to sit down.**

Pass out the noisemakers, then say: **While we're silently holding these, we'll go around the circle and name things or situations that tempt us to do wrong.**

Begin by naming something that tempts you, and have kids continue around the circle. They might name things such as sneaking a dessert, playing video games when they're supposed to be doing homework, lying about doing something wrong, and so on. Pay attention to the noise level and if you hear a child making a sound with his or her noisemaker, silently point to the child and indicate that he or she is to sit down.

When you've gone around the circle, notice how many kids are still standing, and comment on whether this group seems to have a hard time resisting temptation or seems to be able to resist temptation fairly well. Then let all the kids stand and use their noisemakers for one whole minute, making as much noise as possible. Then collect the noisemakers.

Ask: • **What made it hard or easy for you to resist the temptation to use your noisemaker?**

• **Do you think you're usually good at resisting temptation or not? Why?**

• **Why is it sometimes hard to say no to things that we know are wrong?**

Say: **Jesus knows that it's hard to always do what's right and that sometimes doing the wrong thing looks fun. We get tempted to do the wrong thing. Sometimes we're strong enough to say no to the temptation and that's when we do the right thing. Jesus told us that we can ask God to help us when we're tempted to do the wrong thing. The part of the Lord's Prayer that we're learning today says, "And lead us not into temptation." This verse reminds us that 🌑 God can give us strength to do what is right.**

STORY EXCURSION

The Way Out
(15 minutes)

Kids will consider how Bible passages about temptation apply to their lives.

Items to Pack: Bible, 2 pieces of paper, pen

On one piece of paper write "God," and on the other write "Sin." Choose two children and have them stand on either side of you. Give one the God sign and the other the Sin sign to hold up in front of them.

Read James 1:13-15 aloud.

Say: **This verse tells us that God doesn't tempt us. Temptation is what happens between doing right or wrong. For example, if I am looking at God** (turn and face the God sign) **and I'm doing what's right, I am not sinning. What's something that might tempt me to look away from God and stop doing right?** (Have children call out things that might tempt you, and choose one of their ideas.) **If I think about doing this wrong thing, I start to turn away from God.** (Slowly turn your body away from God so you are facing front again.) **I am thinking about whether I should do what is right** (face the God sign) **or what is wrong** (face the Sin sign). **This middle time where I am thinking of whether to do right or wrong is the time that I am being tempted. If I decide to do the wrong thing, I will sin.** (Turn and put your arm around the child holding the Sin sign.) **Or I can decide I don't want to sin and I want to obey God.** (Turn and put your arm around the child holding the God sign.) **The verse we read reminds us that it's our own desires that turn us from God and let us choose sin. God doesn't tempt us. In fact, ◕ God can give us strength so that we don't sin! Let's see what the Bible says about this.**

Have your helpers return to their seats, then read 1 Corinthians 10:13 aloud.

Say: **The Bible says God will provide a "way out" for us when we're tempted. That means that when we're tempted to do wrong, there's always a choice that will let us do what God wants—what is right.**

Have children form groups of four or five. Explain that you're going to read several situations, and the groups will need to determine what the temptation is and what the "way out" is for the child in the story. Read the following scenarios.

Situation 1

Chad was excited about spending the night at Zachary's house with some other guys from school. When it got late, Chris suggested they watch a movie. He brought out Shriek of the Vampire. *Chad's parents didn't want him to watch horror movies. Tyler teased, "Chad can't watch it. He'd be scared!" Chad wanted to watch the movie. His parents probably wouldn't find out anyway. But Chad knew it was wrong to disobey them. He wondered to himself, "What should I do?"*

Have kids discuss what Chad is being tempted to do, and what the "way out" is for Chad. After a few minutes of discussion, have each group share its idea of what Chad should do. Then read the next situation.

Situation 2

Amanda and Sarah always sat together at lunch. Neither one had to worry about sitting alone. Amanda always knew she had a friend, not like Kristen who sat by herself. Kristen was not popular, and most people thought she was kind of annoying.

One day, while Amanda and Sarah were eating, Kristen walked right toward them. Sarah said, "Quick, put your book on that empty seat so she won't sit here."

Have kids discuss what Amanda is being tempted to do, and what the "way out" is for Amanda. After a few minutes of discussion, have each group share its idea of what Amanda should do. Then read the next situation.

Situation 3

Cameron's parents told him he couldn't play any video games until his homework was done and his room was clean. Cameron did clean his room, but then got tired of working and decided he needed a rest. "My parents are in the kitchen talking. They won't know if I play just one video game before I start my homework," he thought.

Have kids discuss what Cameron is being tempted to do, and what the "way out" is for Cameron. After a few minutes of discussion, have each group share its idea of what Cameron should do. Then ask:

• **How does knowing God help us know which actions are right and which are wrong in these situations?**

• **When can we ask God to give us strength?**

Items to Pack: Bible, newsprint, tape, markers

ADVENTURES IN GROWING

(10 minutes)
Temptation Rap

Kids will create actions for a rap and discover that Jesus is ready to help everyone who faces temptation.

Preparation: Write the words to the rap below on newsprint, and post it so everyone can see them.

Read 1 Corinthians 10:13 aloud again. Remind kids that others face the same temptations they do, and that even Jesus faced temptations while he was on earth. Read Hebrews 4:15-16 aloud.

Say: **Jesus is the "high priest" mentioned in this verse. Although Jesus was tempted, he never gave in to temptation or sinned. Since Jesus understands temptation, we can go to him for help whenever we're tempted.**

Have children act out the various situations, then let groups act out their responses as different endings to the situations.

Point out the newsprint with the rap on it. Have kids work together to develop actions to accompany the words. Repeat the rap two or three times.

> Sometimes I feel it's only me
> Who finds it hard as it can be
> To do the things I know I should,
> Avoid the wrong and do the good.
> But others have this trouble too.
> And now I know what I should do!
> When tempted now to go astray,
> I'll look to God, yes, stop and pray.
> I'll ask his help to keep me strong
> And follow his way, all day long.

SCENIC ROUTE → Let kids use the noise-makers or rhythm instruments from the "Noise or Not" activity to accompany their rap.

Ask: • **What do you think tempts a child in another country?**

• **What do you think tempts grown-ups?**

• **What do you think tempts kids in our class?**

• **How can we help each other resist temptation?**

(10 minutes)
On the Curvy and Narrow

Kids will experience the difficulty of following a leader through the midst of many distractions.

Items to Pack: wide masking tape, Bible

Preparation: Mark a winding path on the floor using masking tape.

Choose one child to be the leader and five children to be followers. Remaining kids should position themselves around the room. Only the leader is permitted to look down at the masking tape path on the floor. Followers may look only at the back of the head of the person in front of them. As the leader and followers travel the path, the remaining kids should try to distract the followers. They may call out followers' names or do crazy antics to get them to look away. Repeat the activity so kids experience more than one role, and then discuss the following questions.

Ask: • **Was it hard or easy to ignore the distractions?**

• **Which distractions were the most difficult to ignore?**

• **What things distract us from following Jesus?**

• **How can distractions tempt us to do what's wrong?**

• **How can we help each other stay focused on following him?**

Read aloud Hebrews 12:2-3.

SCENIC ROUTE → Make following the leader even more challenging! Blindfold followers who then must follow the leader by listening for his or her voice. Remaining kids can make noise, imitate the leader's voice, or give conflicting directions in an attempt to distract followers from staying on the path.

Ask: • **How is fixing our eyes on Jesus like fixing our eyes on the head of the person in front of us in the game?**

• **How does keeping our eyes or our attention on Jesus keep us from being tempted to sin?**

SOUVENIRS (10 minutes)

Tackling Temptation Game

Kids will learn how to tackle temptation by pairing temptations with better choices in this game.

Items to Pack: copies of both the Tackling Temptation Playing Board (p. 83) and game cards page (p. 84) for each child, scissors, markers or crayons, envelopes

Give children the handouts, and have them cut out the sixteen cards. Let kids use markers or crayons to create designs on the blank sides of their cards, then explain how to play the game as follows.

1. Find a partner. Each person needs his or her own copy of the Tackling Temptation Playing Board. Only one set of cards is needed for the game, so one child may put his or hers away.

2. Cards are shuffled and placed face down. The youngest child goes first by drawing and reading aloud one card. The child decides how the action on the card can help overcome one of the temptations on the board, and places the card over that temptation. Some cards may be appropriate for more than one temptation, so the child may choose which temptation to cover with those cards.

3. Children take turns playing. The first child to cover four temptations in a row (in any direction—down, across, or diagonal) wins. Cards are shuffled and children may play again with the same partner or a different partner.

When kids are finished playing, distribute envelopes to hold the cards. Remind children to place their Tackling Temptation Games in their Travel Journals.

TOUR GUIDE TIP

Have kids draw the same distinctive pattern on the back of each of their Tackling Temptation Cards to mark their decks as their own.

SCENIC ROUTE

Encourage kids to play the game at home with family members. Can they think of other temptations to tackle and make a bigger playing board?

HOME AGAIN PRAYER (5 minutes)

Strength from God

Have kids pray with their partner from the Tackling Temptations Game. Tell kids to share with their partners one temptation they face that they need God's strength to resist. They can refer to their games if they need ideas. Give partners time to pray, then close with this group prayer.

Pray: **Dear Lord, thank you for promising to provide a way out when we are tempted to do wrong. Help us recognize temptations that pull us away from you and remember you can give us strength to do what's right. In Jesus' name we pray. Amen.**

Tackling Temptation
Playing Board

Sometimes I am tempted to **stay outside too late.**	Sometimes I am tempted to **copy from someone else's homework.**	Sometimes I am tempted to **stay home from church to play.**	Sometimes I am tempted to **take a candy bar that isn't mine.**
Sometimes I am tempted to **make fun of someone who is different.**	Sometimes I am tempted to **use bad language when I'm angry.**	Sometimes I am tempted to **blame my friend for my own mistake.**	Sometimes I am tempted to **copy answers from someone else's test.**
Sometimes I am tempted to **laugh when someone is being teased.**	Sometimes I am tempted to **eat a cookie when Dad said wait 'til later.**	Sometimes I am tempted to **watch a TV show Mom said not to watch.**	Sometimes I am tempted to **hide my toys under my bed when Dad says to clean up.**
Sometimes I am tempted to **cheat when playing a game.**	Sometimes I am tempted to **make fun of my teacher when he or she isn't looking.**	Sometimes I am tempted to **poke my brother in the ribs, then say he poked me first.**	Sometimes I am tempted to **be rude to my teacher.**

Our Father in heaven, hallowed be your name, your kingdom come, your will be done on earth as it is in heaven. Give us today our daily bread. Forgive us our debts, as we also have forgiven our debtors. **And lead us not into temptation** (MATTHEW 6:9B-13A).

Game Cards

God can give me strength to **be inside on time.**	God can give me strength to **turn off the TV and do my homework.**	God can give me strength to **go to church now and play later.**	God can give me strength to **save my allowance to buy a candy bar.**
God can give me strength to **be kind to others, even if it's hard.**	God can give me strength to **use kind words.**	God can give me strength to **admit when I'm wrong.**	God can give me strength to **study for my test.**
God can give me strength to **stand up for those who are being teased.**	God can give me strength to **wait 'til after dinner to have dessert.**	God can give me strength to **obey when Mom says to turn off the TV.**	God can give me strength to **clean my room when asked.**
God can give me strength to **follow the rules to games.**	God can give me strength to **show respect to adults.**	God can give me strength to **show kindness to my brother.**	God can give me strength to **be polite to my teacher.**

But Deliver Us From the Evil One
(Matthew 6:13b)

Pathway Point: 🌀 God can protect us.

In-Focus Verse: "But deliver us from the evil one" (Matthew 6:13b).

Travel Itinerary

Kids often think of the devil as a mean-looking caricature with horns, tail, and pitchfork, little more than a Halloween costume choice. To be protected from spiritual harm, kids need to know we have a very real enemy trying to destroy our faith. An important part of their defense is learning to recognize activities that can lead them away from God and into Satan's influence.

Unfortunately, evil activities once condemned by our culture are now gaining acceptance. Witchcraft, spiritism, pagan religions, and occult practices are increasingly viewed as nothing more than alternative forms of spiritual expression or even harmless games. However, involvement with satanic influences can endanger a believer's faith. Lead kids to recognize that God can protect us, and instill in them the confidence that the battle has already been won by Jesus!

TOUR GUIDE TIP

The activities in this book have been designed for multi-age groups. Select from the activities, or adapt them as needed for your class.

DEPARTURE PRAYER

(5 minutes)

Have kids stand shoulder to shoulder in a tight circle, facing outward, with their arms crossed in front of them.

Say: **If we were in a battle against a terrible enemy, we'd do everything possible to shield ourselves from the attack. We could stand close together like this and let our arms shield us.**

Jesus knows that we face an enemy who tries to destroy our faith. In the Lord's Prayer, he taught us to pray, "but deliver us from the evil one." As we pray, let's continue to stand as if we're shielding ourselves from danger. Let's begin by saying what we know of the Lord's Prayer so far, then I'll close our prayer.

Pray: **Our Father in heaven, hallowed be your name, your kingdom come, your will be done on earth as it is in heaven. Give us today our daily bread. Forgive us our debts, as we also have forgiven our debtors. And lead us not into temptation.**

Dear Lord, when you taught your followers to pray, you encouraged them to ask for protection from the evil one. Give us wisdom to recognize

TOUR GUIDE TIP

This lesson does not shy away from the fact that Satan and his evil ways are real. Be clear that your intent is not to frighten children, but to encourage them to look to God for strength and protection.

the evil influences the devil uses to hurt us. Help us avoid evil and trust you to protect us. Amen.

STOP 1st DISCOVERY (10 minutes)
Protect Me!

Kids will dodge "evil influences" and learn the value of being shielded from evil.

Preparation: Use masking tape to mark two team lines twelve feet apart.

Help kids brainstorm a list of things Satan might use to hurt us. Some examples are séances, psychics, witchcraft, spells, Ouija boards, or fortunetelling. Also encourage kids to think of life experiences the devil might use to lead a person to abandon his faith, such as doubt, sadness, or persecution. As the kids call out their ideas, drop one pingpong ball for each idea into a basket. Explain that each ball will represent one of Satan's hurtful ways.

Say: **In our game, you're going to try to keep from being hit by these evil tricks of Satan.**

Have the children form two teams, and ask teams to stand behind the masking tape lines. Divide the balls evenly among one team's members so that each child has at least two balls. At your signal, have the team with the balls throw them at the opposite team while the other team members try to avoid being hit. Gather and distribute the balls to the second team, reversing roles so each team has an opportunity to be both throwers and defenders.

Ask: • **What made it hard to dodge the balls?**

• **What would help your team avoid getting hit by all these evil influences?**

Play the game again, but this time provide the defending team with two plastic trash-can lids to use as shields. As before, let both teams have a chance to be both throwers and defenders.

Gather the playing items, and have kids return to their seats.

Ask: • **How did you feel when the balls came flying toward you this time?**

• **What difference did it make to have a shield?**

• **How did having only two shields affect the way your team worked together?**

• **How can God be like a shield to protect us from evil?**

Say: Satan uses all sorts of evil tricks to try to discourage, mislead, or harm people. Sometimes it seems as if evil influences are flying all around us. But ⬤ God can protect us. He does not leave us defenseless, but provides us with protective armor and a spiritual shield to keep us safe.

Items to Pack: pingpong balls, masking tape, basket, 2 plastic trash-can lids

TOUR GUIDE TIP
If you don't have access to trash-can lids, use umbrellas or large pieces of cardboard as shields. Remind kids to play carefully and avoid injuring others with the pointed spokes of the umbrellas.

TOUR GUIDE TIP
If pingpong balls are not available, use paper balls instead. Let kids crumple paper into balls and toss them into the basket as they brainstorm ways Satan tries to hurt us.

TOUR GUIDE TIP
As kids use the shields, help them discover how they can work together to protect the greatest number of kids with only two shields.

(15 minutes)

Armor for Millennial Kids

Kids will consider the spiritual armor that God gives Christians.

Items to Pack: Bible

Have children form six groups, mixing older children with younger ones.

Say: **In our game we used shields as armor to protect us. The Bible tells us about a full set of armor God provides to protect us. We call this the armor of God.**

Read Ephesians 6:10-17 aloud. Assign each group one piece of armor to consider and present to the class.

The six pieces of armor are

• the belt of truth,

• the breastplate of righteousness,

• the footwear of the readiness that comes from the gospel of peace,

• the shield of faith,

• the helmet of salvation, and

• the sword of the Spirit.

In their groups, have kids discuss these questions.

• How does your piece of armor protect a warrior in battle?

• How does adding something from God to this piece of armor protect us in a war against evil?

Groups should also choose a piece of contemporary clothing or an accessory someone in their group is already wearing that would be similar to their part of God's armor. Allow time for kids to discuss, assisting groups as needed.

Have each group report what they discussed about the protective nature of their piece of armor and what a current comparison might be. If you choose to make additional comments about the pieces of armor, wait until the group has finished sharing before adding your thoughts.

Ask: **• What part of God's armor have you used most often?**

• What part have you used the least?

• How do these pieces of armor work together to protect us?

Say: **God is stronger than our enemy and** 🌍 **God can protect us. That is why he provides us with spiritual armor. When we wear God's armor, we can be confident that God will "deliver us from the evil one."**

TOUR GUIDE TIP

If children are not sure what a breastplate is, explain that it was the piece of armor that covered the chest.

SCENIC ROUTE →

Invite a police officer or firefighter to visit and show the equipment he or she wears for protection. How does the "armor" of this modern-day warrior compare with the armor of God?

SCENIC ROUTE →

Provide a collection of headgear, footwear, clothing, and accessories kids can choose from to represent their contemporary pieces of God's armor. Include helmets (baseball, bike, fire, or motorcycle), footwear (boots, sandals, or sneakers), trash-can lids or umbrellas, army or hunting vests, belts, and protective sports equipment such as football pads or baseball catcher gear.

Items to Pack: Bible, poster board, markers

TOUR GUIDE TIP If you have older children in your class, let them take turns reading the verses aloud to the others.

TOUR GUIDE TIP You may think these situations are unrealistic for children in your church, but if you visit any toy store or large bookstore, you'll find Ouija boards right beside games such as Monopoly and Candyland, and you'll find books of spells and incantations for children in bright colors.

ADVENTURES IN GROWING

(15 minutes)
Where Do You Stand?

Kids will evaluate activities to determine if they lead us closer to God or closer to evil.

Preparation: Use the poster board and markers to make a sign that reads "God."

Choose a child to stand in the middle of the room and hold the sign. Explain that this child will need to stay in this spot, while the others move according to the activity. Have all the children begin standing very close to the child with the "God" sign.

Say: **Let's think about how our choices influence our relationships with God. Some things we do lead us closer to God, while others lead us away from God and toward evil. First, I'll read a description of an activity. Think about whether it might lead that person closer to God or farther from God. Choose a place to stand in the room that's either close to God or far from God. If you are touching any wall, that will be the farthest you can get from God, and that will represent evil. Next, I will read a Bible verse. If it changes how you think about where you're standing, you may move to a new location.**

Read the following examples, allowing time for children to choose their positions in the room. Then read the verse, allowing kids to change positions if they desire.

Tanya's friend Emily loved to sing along with songs on the radio, so Tanya invited Emily to join her for choir practice at church. Read aloud Colossians 3:16.

Madison went to a sleepover. That night the girls had a séance. They turned off the lights, held hands, and tried to get a dead person to talk to them or show them a sign. Read aloud Isaiah 8:19-20.

Sammy dreaded seeing Eric. Eric called him a loser and shoved him when no one was watching. One day, Sammy saw a book of magic spells. It said "Spells for every occasion! Amaze your friends! Conquer your enemies!" He wondered if they might work on Eric. Read aloud Deuteronomy 18:10-12.

Sometimes Kaitlyn worried about the devil and how he might try to harm her. So she prayed about her worries and memorized a Bible verse about God's power. Read aloud 1 John 4:4.

Janice's mom bought her a CD that had a lot of songs on it that told how great God is. Janice started listening to this before she went to school each day. Read aloud Philippians 4:8.

Pete learned at church that God wants to protect us from evil. He wondered if it was OK to play his video game with gunmen and snipers. Read aloud 1 Thessalonians 5:22.

James watched a movie in which the kids used bad language and talked back to their parents. During an argument the next day, James used some of the same words. Read aloud Ephesians 4:29.

Jessica was watching TV when she saw a commercial for a psychic hotline. It said the psychic could tell your future. Jessica's Aunt Cathy said, "I'd love to find out about my future." Read aloud Leviticus 19:31.

Micah watched his dad help disabled kids at Special Olympics. He patiently helped kids get ready to race and cheered like crazy when they crossed the finish line. Micah thought, "When I grow up, I want to be like my dad." Read aloud 3 John 11.

Melissa's friends were going to a haunted house on Halloween night. Haunted houses made her feel creepy. She knew it was pretend, but she still felt scared. Read aloud 2 Thessalonians 3:3.

Gather the group back together.

Ask: • How can we tell if something will lead you closer to God or farther from him?

• If you changed positions after hearing the Bible verse, why did you change?

• What should we do if things that lead away from God still seem interesting or fun?

• How can we help each other avoid evil?

Say: To stay spiritually safe, we want to enjoy lots of activities that lead us closer to God, such as being with other Christians, praying, studying the Bible, and serving others. God can help us avoid evil things that lead us away from him. When there is so much evil around us, it's great to know that 🌀 God can protect us.

TOUR GUIDE TIP Refrain from making judgments on the children's choices. Let them hear what God's Word says about the choices they make.

TOUR GUIDE TIP With world events opening our eyes to the evil actions of others, children may want to discuss why God allows bad things to happen. Obviously there are Christians who die in war, famines, terrorist attacks, and so on. Assure children that God still protects the souls of these people, taking them to heaven to be with him. And God often uses these times of pain to bring us closer to him. There are no easy answers, but do allow children to share their fears and concerns as you assure them of God's love and power.

(10 minutes)
Shield of Faith

Children will design shields of faith to remind them of God's protection.

Items to Pack: ½ sheet of poster board per child, newsprint, scissors, markers, stickers (optional)

Preparation: Before class, cut pieces of poster board in half, and cut oval-shaped handles in the middle of each "shield." Write the following Bible verses on newsprint, and post it so kids can copy verses onto their shields.

"The Lord your God is with you, he is mighty to save" (Zephaniah 3:17a).

SCENIC ROUTE → After kids have made their shields, use them to play the "Protect Me!" activity again.

SCENIC ROUTE → If time permits, provide glue and other decorating materials, such as glitter, fabric scraps, colored paper, and so on, for children to add to their shields.

Items to Pack: copies of the "Roaring Lion" handout (p. 92), markers or crayons

TOUR GUIDE TIP Make a sample project, and practice the folding instructions so you can confidently demonstrate the technique for kids.

FUN FACT Did you know that lions do not have to eat every day? They average only twenty kills a year, but they may eat sixty-five pounds of meat in a single meal!

"God is our refuge and strength, an ever-present help in trouble" (Psalm 46:1).

"Be strong in the Lord and in his mighty power" (Ephesians 6:10).

"But deliver us from the evil one" (Matthew 6:13b).

Say: **There are many ways ⬤ God can protect us from evil. One is the shield of faith, part of the armor of God we learned about earlier. Let's create shields with symbols that remind us of God's protection and a Bible verse that tells of his power. You may choose one or more of the verses posted on the newsprint to include on your shield.**

Give kids time to work on the shields, drawing symbols, adding stickers (if provided), and adding Bible verses. Encourage older kids to help younger ones with lettering if needed.

SOUVENIRS → (10 minutes)
Roaring Lion Poster

Kids will personalize a folding poster to remind them that Jesus has conquered the devil and promises to protect us from evil.

Read 1 Peter 5:8b aloud.

Say: **This verse compares Satan to a lion hunting for prey to eat. Lions are dangerous, and we don't want to be near them! Our activity will remind us that Jesus is stronger than Satan and stands between us and evil.**

Have children color the lion and Jesus as they like, and draw a picture of themselves in the blank area on the right side of the page. Then demonstrate how to fold the page. Fold along both dotted lines, folding these areas back from the picture of Jesus. Then bring the two folds together. This will put the lion right next to the drawing of the child, and allow children only to see the growling of the lion. When children spread the page apart again, they'll see that Jesus stands between them and the evil of Satan.

When all have finished their projects, say: **Although Satan is a very real enemy, Jesus has already conquered him by his death and resurrection. As we trust in Jesus, ⬤ God can protect us from evil.**

Remind kids to put completed posters in their Travel Journals.

(5 minutes)
Wearing the Armor

Gather kids in a circle.

Say: **As we pray today, we'll remember the armor God gives us. As I mention each piece of armor, pretend that you're putting it on, piece by piece. For example, when I mention the belt of truth, pretend you are putting a belt around your waist.**

As you pray, pause at the appropriate times to allow kids to act out each part.

Pray: **Dear God, thank you for sending Jesus to conquer evil for us. Thank you for giving us the armor of God. Thank you for the belt of truth. Thank you for the breastplate of righteousness. Thank you for the shoes of being ready to share the gospel of peace. Thank you for the shield of faith. Thank you for the helmet of salvation. Thank you for the sword of the Spirit, which is the Word of God. Help us to remember to wear this armor every day so you can protect us from evil. Amen.**

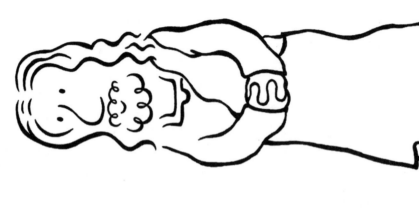

Roaring Lion

...eater is he that is in me...

...than he that is in the world" (1 John 4:4, LB)

G r r r r r

"Your enemy the devil prowls around like a roaring lion looking for someone to devour" (1 Peter 5:8b)

"Our Father in heaven, hallowed be your name, your kingdom come, your will be done on earth as it is in heaven. Give us today our daily bread. Forgive us our debts, as we also have forgiven our debtors. And lead us not into temptation, **but deliver us from the evil one"** (Matthew 6:9b-13).

Reviewing the Lord's Prayer

Pathway Point: ◗ We can always talk to God.

In-Focus Verse: the Lord's Prayer (Matthew 6:9-13)

Travel Itinerary

Kids have spent the last weeks considering each part of the Lord's Prayer. Now it is time to put the parts together as a whole. Jesus taught the Lord's Prayer to his disciples as a model for prayer. Both spiritual and physical needs are addressed in its petitions. Going beyond rote recitation of the prayer, kids will understand what Jesus encourages us to communicate with God through prayer.

In this lesson kids will review the Pathway Points they have learned in previous lessons and will continue to incorporate the Lord's Prayer into their lives as an ongoing part of their relationships with God.

TOUR GUIDE TIP The activities in this book have been designed for multi-age groups. Select from the activities, or adapt them as needed for your class.

DEPARTURE PRAYER (5 minutes)

Say: **We've taken a lot of time learning each part of the Lord's Prayer. Let's begin our time today by saying it all together. Most people finish this prayer by saying, "For yours is the kingdom and the power and the glory forever. Amen." This isn't included in all Bibles, but it's a tradition most churches use to conclude the Lord's Prayer, so we'll end ours that way today.**

Pray: **Our Father in heaven, hallowed be your name, your kingdom come, your will be done on earth as it is in heaven. Give us today our daily bread. Forgive us our debts, as we also have forgiven our debtors. And lead us not into temptation, but deliver us from the evil one. For yours is the kingdom and the power and the glory forever. Amen.**

1st STOP DISCOVERY (15 minutes)
Prayer Toss

Kids will play a beanbag game and review Pathway Points from the previous lessons.

Items to Pack: beanbag for each child, nine 8-inch square pieces of paper, markers, tape

Preparation: Before kids arrive, write the Pathway Points from Lessons 3-11 on nine 8-inch squares of paper. The Pathway Points are as follows:

God is our heavenly Father who hears our prayers.

TOUR GUIDE TIP If your group is large, make two or more playing areas so kids can play in groups of ten or less.

TOUR GUIDE TIP If you're unable to locate enough beanbags for this game, fill snack-sized self-sealing bags with dried beans or rice. Seal them well (you might even want to add tape to be sure the seal is secure) and use these for the game.

We can worship God through prayer.

We can be a part of God's kingdom.

God's desires and plans should guide our prayers.

We can ask God to provide for our needs.

We can ask God for forgiveness.

God asks us to forgive others.

God can give us strength.

God can protect us.

Use these squares to form a grid on the floor, three squares wide by three squares long. Secure each square to the floor with tape.

Have children stand in a circle around the playing area. Give each child a beanbag.

Say: **We've learned about each part of the Lord's Prayer, which is a prayer Jesus gave his followers as an example to follow. Our game area has squares with each week's Pathway Point. Listen as I read some stories. Think how the Lord's Prayer might apply to each situation. Toss your beanbag onto a Pathway Point you think applies to the situation.**

Read the following situations aloud. After each situation is read, allow kids to toss their beanbags. Let kids tell why they chose various Pathway Points, and help kids see that more than one may apply. Tell kids to pick up their beanbags before beginning the next situation.

• Mom and Dad were busy outside when Jenna heard a commercial on TV about a lady who could tell the future. You could talk to her by calling a phone number.

• Jason loved playing Jeremy's video game. It was an old one that Jeremy hardly ever played. Jason thought, "I could slip it in my pocket when he's not looking. He probably wouldn't even miss it."

• Playing basketball used to be fun, but lately Brenna and Tony were arguing more than playing. Each accused the other of cheating, and they often went home angry.

• Chase climbed up the willow tree in his back yard. It was a perfect summer day. There was nothing he had to do and nowhere he had to go. The whole wonderful summer stretched out in front of him. Chase decided he would talk to God from his perch in the tree.

• Madison studied for the math test but still didn't think she would get a good grade. Maybe she'd take a quick glance at Matt's paper, just to check her answers.

• Katie was furious at her mom. She yelled, "I wish you weren't my mom!" Later on, she felt terrible. She didn't really mean it. Katie knew she had hurt her mom's feelings.

• Amy was lonely after her best friend moved away. She missed having someone to talk to, someone who would listen and care.

• Jessica was angry when she found out her best friend, Kelly, had told a lie about her. When Kelly called to say she was sorry, Jessica wasn't sure what to do.

• The Valdez family's stories of mission work in Guatemala made Brandon want to be a missionary too. Perhaps someday he would. Until then, he could share God's love by inviting neighborhood friends to church.

• LeShawn was listening to the radio when a song about God's power came on. She decided to sing the song to God.

• Christine's mom and dad called a family meeting. Dad had been offered a new job in another city. He said, "This looks like a great opportunity, but we don't want to make this decision on our own. Let's pray and ask God to guide us."

• Caroline's mother lost her job. Her parents seemed sad, and at night she could hear their worried voices. Sometimes Caroline worried too. Would Mom be able to find a new job?

Gather the beanbags, and have children return to their seats.

Ask: • How do these lessons we've learned help us when we pray?

• Why might people think of different parts of the Lord's Prayer for the same situation?

Say: The Lord's Prayer relates to our lives today. This prayer helps us understand that 🌀 we can always talk to God about anything!

SCENIC ROUTE → Invite a missionary to speak about how important prayer is in his or her ministry. Pray together for the missionary's needs, and give kids a list of the mission's prayer concerns for families to use at home.

STORY EXCURSION (10 minutes)
Teach Us to Pray

Kids will review the story of Jesus' teaching the Lord's Prayer and create actions to help them remember and experience the prayer's different parts.

Items to Pack: Bible, newsprint, marker, tape

Preparation: Before children arrive, write the words of the Lord's Prayer on the newsprint, and tape it to the wall.

Read Matthew 6:9-13 aloud.

Say: Jesus taught his followers the Lord's Prayer as an example to help them know how to pray. The prayer wasn't just for those followers; it's for

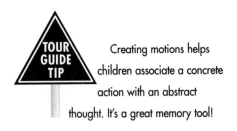

us, too. Jesus taught this prayer to show we can always talk to God. The Lord's Prayer is such an important example, we want to learn it well. To help us keep it in our hearts, let's create actions to go with each part.

Read the words to the Lord's Prayer together, breaking the prayer into many sections. As a group, create actions for each section. When kids are finished, use the words and actions to pray the Lord's Prayer together. Repeat this several times so kids are familiar with the actions.

Items to Pack: Bibles, paper, pencils or pens

(10 minutes)
Say It Again

Children will rephrase verses about prayer.

Have children form four groups. Assign each group one of the following verses:
- Philippians 4:6
- 1 Thessalonians 5:16-18
- Colossians 4:2
- James 5:13

Say: **In your groups, read your verse aloud. Then rewrite the verse in your own words. Work together so that everyone understands the words in the verse and helps to think of new words to express the same meaning.**

After about five minutes, have a representative from each group read their verse from the Bible, then read their paraphrase.

Ask: • **What do these verses teach us about prayer?**

• **How do these verses remind us of what we've learned from the Lord's Prayer?**

• **Why do you think the Bible says so much about prayer?**

Say: **There are many places in the Bible where people talk to God, and many places where we are taught to talk to God. The Bible tells us how important it is to talk to God.**

SCENIC ROUTE →

Teach kids to PRAY! Use this acronym to help kids broaden their prayers. P–Praise! R–Repent! A–Another's needs! Y–Your needs!

Items to Pack: newspaper, globe, several canned food items, first-aid kit, photo of your pastor, Bible

ADVENTURES IN GROWING

(15 minutes)
Prayer Journey

Kids will move to different locations in your room and pray as guided by different items.

Preparation: Place each of the items for the Prayer Journey in a different location in your room.

Form travel groups of three to five. Have each group choose one child to be the Navigator. The Navigator's job is to guide the group to all six stations. Let groups choose another child to be the Reporter. The Reporter's job is to help the group choose a favorite station. Travel groups will report to the large group on their favorite station. One child in each group will be the Director. The Director makes sure that each person has a turn to lead a prayer.

Say: **We're going on a Prayer Journey. The Navigator will guide you to each prayer station. Navigators, try to spread out so all the groups are not at the same prayer station at the same time.**

When you get to a prayer station, talk about the item located there, and discuss the prayer concerns it brings to mind. The Director will ask a different person at each station to choose one idea and lead the group in a short prayer. After praying, move to the next station. The Reporter will help your group decide which station you liked best and remember your prayer topic there.

Help groups begin at different stations, and have them proceed until they've completed all the stations.

When all the groups have finished, have children return to their seats, and let each group's Reporter share about his or her group's favorite station.

Say: **Even when we look at the same situation, we may think of different things to pray about. It's good when people bring different prayer needs to God. Every day we have experiences that give us ideas for prayer. If you see a child crying, or hear emergency-vehicle sirens, you can pray. If someone shares an answer to prayer, or if you discover a reason to praise God, tell him about it! All these experiences remind us 🌓 we can always talk to God.**

SOUVENIRS → (10 minutes)
Pray All Day

Kids will design a clock face to remind them of topics for prayer encouraged in the Bible.

Provide scissors for kids to cut out the clock hands. Demonstrate how to attach the hands to the clock using a brad.

Say: **The Bible encourages us to pray for many things and many people. Some of these Bible verses are next to the clock. On the lines near the Bible verse, add the names of specific**

SCENIC ROUTE → If you have the use of more than one classroom, spread your Prayer Journey through several rooms. Create a simple map for children to follow, and have them travel through various areas of your building to find different stations for prayer.

TOUR GUIDE TIP Make the locations for prayer more visible within your classroom by writing the numbers 1 through 6 on sheets of paper and posting them over the Prayer Journey items.

TOUR GUIDE TIP Encourage children to consider the items at each prayer station to spark ideas for prayers. If children are still unsure what to pray for, suggest people who are in the news for the newspaper, people around the world for the globe, people who are in need of food or jobs for the canned food, people who are sick for the first-aid kit, your pastor and church leaders for the photograph, and thanking God for communicating with us for the Bible.

Items to Pack: copy of the "Time to Pray" page (p. 99) for each child, scissors, markers, 1 brad per child

people you would like to pray for. For example, the topic at one o'clock reads, "Government leaders, 1 Timothy 2:1-2." At one o'clock we might pray for the president, our governor, or someone who works in the government. Write the name of the person you would like to pray for on the line under the Bible verse.

Read each hour's prayer topic and verse reference. Give kids time to fill in the blanks and decorate the clocks with markers as they like. Remind kids to place their completed clocks in their Travel Journals.

HOME AGAIN PRAYER (5 minutes)
The Lord's Prayer

Say: Let's close by praying the Lord's Prayer together. After we pray each line, we'll pause. During that time, talk to God silently about what that phrase means to you. When I continue with the next line, please join with me in praying it aloud.

If you like, have children also use the motions they created earlier in the lesson to accompany this prayer.

Pray: **Our Father in heaven, hallowed be your name, your kingdom come, your will be done on earth as it is in heaven. Give us today our daily bread. Forgive us our debts, as we also have forgiven our debtors. And lead us not into temptation, but deliver us from the evil one, for yours is the kingdom and the power and the glory forever. Amen.**

TOUR GUIDE TIP Use newsprint to post the names of people kids might use to personalize their clocks. Include the names of government workers in your congregation, missionaries supported by your church, and the names of ill friends or family members known to your children. Find out more about persecuted Christians and how to specifically pray for them at the Web sites for Voice of the Martyrs (www.persecution.com) and the International Day of Prayer for the Persecuted Church (www.persecutedchurch.org).

SCENIC ROUTE → Provide children with old magazines and glue sticks. Encourage kids to find pictures representing people who need prayer. Cut them out and glue them to the clock face as a reminder to pray.

SCENIC ROUTE → Invite one of your church's lay leaders to talk about your congregation's prayer needs. Encourage kids to place this leader's name on their prayer clock.

Time to Pray

PRAY CONTINUALLY
(1 THESSALONIANS 5:17)

I CAN PRAY FOR...

1. Government leaders (1 Timothy 2:1-2)

2. Other Christians (Ephesians 6:18)

3. Guidance in my own life (Isaiah 55:6)

4. Those who mistreat me (Luke 6:28)

5. Those who are sick (James 5:14)

6. Myself to not give in to temptation (Luke 22:40)

7. Those in trouble (James 5:13)

8. More people to tell others about God (Matthew 9:38)

9. Myself to tell others about God (Philemon 6)

10. Those who are mistreated because of what they believe (Hebrews 13:3)

11. Leaders of the church (Acts 6:6-7)

12. Myself to live a life that pleases God (Colossians 1:10)

How Do I Know If God Heard My Prayer?

Pathway Point: 🌀 God answers all our prayers.

In-Focus Verse: "The Lord will hear when I call to him" (Psalm 4:3b).

Travel Itinerary

Children (and adults!) may have a hard time understanding that God hears our prayers when they don't see immediate results. If God doesn't answer our prayers in the way we desire, does that mean he didn't hear? Or that he doesn't care? Even King David struggled with impatience, pleading with God to answer his prayers.

Use this lesson as a reminder that God does hear us, and God does answer us—even if his answers are not in line with our desires.

DEPARTURE PRAYER (5 minutes)

Have the children keep their eyes open as they join you in the motions used in your prayer.

Pray: **Dear God, thank you for hearing us each time we talk to you.** *(Point to your ears.)* **Help us to remember that you hear when we call to you. Teach us to have faith to wait for you** *(point to your wristwatch)* **to answer us. Teach us to have faith to look for your answer** *(point to eyes)* **and then teach us to have faith to accept the answer you give us** *(point to heart).* **Help us grow in our faith and in our prayer life. Help us to remember that you answer all prayers.**

1st STOP DISCOVERY (10 minutes)
The Answer Is...

Children will consider reasons to not answer "yes" to every question.

Say: **Let's pretend that you're the parents and I'm your child. I'm going to ask you questions about things I want to do. Instead of telling me "yes," "no," or "later on," you have to show me your answer. If your answer is "yes," stand up. If the answer is "no," sit down. If you think I should wait, crouch down.**

Have children spread out around the room so everyone has room to show

---

TOUR GUIDE TIP
The activities in this book have been designed for multi-age groups. Select from the activities, or adapt them as needed for your class.

TOUR GUIDE TIP
Before you start 1st Stop Discovery, ask children how God answers them and how they know that God has heard their prayers.

SCENIC ROUTE →
Have pillows, Bibles, and snacks at a center, and ask the children to sit on the pillows, holding a Bible and a snack. Talk about how we usually think of prayer for bedtime, church, or meals, but that prayer is really meant to be part of our entire lives, not just at certain times.

SCENIC ROUTE →
Ask your church leaders for the use of a corner space or small room as a permanent church prayer space. Have the children clean the area; make or find pictures to decorate the walls; and supply Bibles, paper, and pencils. Give the children a chance to use their prayer place after it has been set up and to change the decorations often to give them a sense of ownership.

their answers. Remind kids that their answers can be different from others in the class.

Ask: • **Mommy and Daddy, can I go swimming by myself?**

Let children show their responses by their body positions, then ask a few of them why they chose their answers. For example, a child might think you're not old enough to swim by yourself, so would say you have to wait, or a child might say yes to your question. Continue the game with the following questions, stopping after children have indicated their responses to let a few of them tell why they chose that answer.

Ask: • **May I cook supper by myself?**

• **Can I get a puppy?**

• **May I stay up late tonight?**

• **Would it be OK if I took your new car out for a drive?**

• **Can I stay home without a baby sitter?**

• **Will you give me a bigger allowance?**

Have all the children return to their seats.

Ask: • **Which of these questions have you asked your parents?**

• **What responses have you gotten from them?**

• **Why do you think parents tell us "yes" sometimes, "no" sometimes, and to "wait until later" or even until we're older sometimes?**

• **How are these questions we ask our parents like things we ask God for?**

• **Do you think God gets tired of us asking for things? Why or why not?**

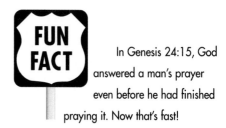

Say: As we've studied the Lord's Prayer, we've learned there are many reasons to pray. But sometimes it seems like God doesn't give us the things we want, or it might seem like God doesn't hear us. This game helps us understand that 🌓 God always answers our prayers, but God's answer might not be what we wanted to hear. Like our parents, God can answer us "yes," "no," or "wait." We can find examples of these answers in the Bible.

STORY EXCURSION (15 minutes)
God's Answers

Children will look in their Bibles for examples of how God answers prayers.

Say: The Bible tells us how God has answered other people's prayers. We're going to do some exploring in our Bibles to learn more about how God answers prayers.

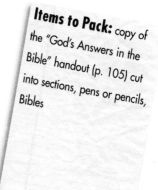

Items to Pack: copy of the "God's Answers in the Bible" handout (p. 105) cut into sections, pens or pencils, Bibles

TOUR GUIDE TIP

Be sure to mix older children who can read and write with younger ones in your groups.

TOUR GUIDE TIP

If you have more than twenty-five children in your class, create extra copies of the handout, and have several groups do the same section of Scripture.

Items to Pack: Bible

Have children form five groups. Give each group one of the sections from the "God's Answers in the Bible" handout, a Bible, and a pen to record their answers on their paper. Allow children time to read the Bible verses as instructed, and to discuss their questions.

After children have had time to discuss these Bible stories, have one child from each group report what they learned. Then say: **God answered each prayer that we read about. Some of the prayers God answered quickly and with the answer of "yes." Some prayers God heard and required people to wait before changing the situation. And there were other prayers that God answered with "no." We don't know why God answers our prayers differently. We have to trust God to control our lives and answer our prayers with his perfect wisdom.**

ADVENTURES IN GROWING

(10 minutes)
Head and Shoulders

Kids will sing a song that represents taking our cares to God.

Sing the song "Head and Shoulders" with the kids, having them point to the appropriate body parts as they sing.

Head and shoulders, knees and toes, knees and toes,
Head and shoulders, knees and toes, knees and toes,
And eyes and ears and mouth and nose,
Head and shoulders, knees and toes, knees and toes.

Say: **This song is a good reminder for us as we pray. "Head" can remind us to think of God while we pray. "Shoulders" can remind us to give our problems to God and get them off our shoulders. "Knees" reminds us to come humbly to God or to bow to him when we pray, and "toes" reminds us to walk with God, or have a relationship with him. Then we look and listen for God's answer** (point to your eyes and ears), **praise God no matter what he answers** (point to your mouth), **and take a deep breath** (point to your nose) **to begin praying again.**

Sing the song together again, with motions, and encourage kids to think about how the words of the song encourage them to pray. Then have children sit down.

Ask: • **This song has so many motions it's like doing exercise. How is prayer like exercise?**

• **Why is our response to God's answer important?**

• **What should you do when God doesn't answer quickly or in the way you wanted?**

Read Luke 18:1-7.

Say: **Just as the woman in the story was persistent, we can be persistent in prayer. God wants us to pray, to exercise our spiritual muscles, and grow stronger in faith and obedience. Remember, to exercise our faith, we need to pray constantly.**

(10 minutes)
My Prayers

Have children return to the first page of their Travel Journals and see what prayers they have written over the past weeks and months. If children have not tracked their prayers through their journals, encourage them to think about what they've been praying about over the past two months.

Have children form small groups and share how God has answered their specific prayers. Has God answered with "yes," "no," or "wait until later"? How do the children know their prayers have been answered?

After time for discussion, invite several children to share with the entire group. Ask for a child who has had a "yes" answer to share, a child who has had a "no" answer to share, and a child who thinks God might be telling him or her to "wait" to also share.

Say: **We know when God has said "yes," and we can usually tell when he's said "no" as well. It's harder when we aren't sure and have to wait for God's answer. But we can be sure that God hears our prayers and that**  **God answers all our prayers.**

 (10 minutes)
Prayer Never Ends

Children will complete their Travel Journals with a reminder to pray continually.

Give children the handouts and drawing supplies. Have them draw praying hands in the section labeled "I pray." Have them draw God or a mouth in the section that says "God answers." Have them draw themselves listening or an ear in the section that says "I listen," and put a heart in the section that says "God treasures my prayer." As children work, read Psalm 4:3b aloud.

Say: **Last week our souvenir page reminded us of 1 Thessalonians 5:17. This is a short verse that says, "Pray continually." As we talk to God all through the day and in the evening, we know that God hears us and that** 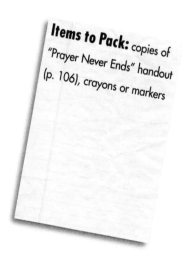 **God answers all our prayers. The circles on this page never end—they** keep on going. That's a reminder to us that our prayers never have to end. We can always be praying and knowing that God is always listening and answering us.

Have children put these pages into their Travel Journals, and remind them to take their journals home with them at the end of class today.

HOME AGAIN PRAYER | (5 minutes)
A Final Prayer

Say: We've learned a lot about prayer over the past weeks. I'll pray, then let's close our time by saying the Lord's Prayer together.

Pray: Dear God, we praise and thank you for hearing and answering our prayers. We ask that you use our prayers to help us grow in our faith and to help change the world.

Together pray: Our Father in heaven, hallowed be your name, your kingdom come, your will be done on earth as it is in heaven. Give us today our daily bread. Forgive us our debts, as we also have forgiven our debtors. And lead us not into temptation, but deliver us from the evil one, for yours is the kingdom and the power and the glory forever. Amen.

God's Answers in the Bible

Group 1

Read 1 Samuel 1:9-11 to find out what Hannah prayed about. Then read 1 Samuel 1:20 for God's answer.

Discuss the following questions in your group:

• What did Hannah want God to give her?

• How did God answer?

• How do you think Hannah felt when God answered her prayer?

Group 2

Read 1 Kings 18:36-37 to find out what Elijah prayed. Then read 1 Kings 18:38-39 to find God's answer.

Discuss the following questions in your group:

• What request did Elijah make to God?

• How did God answer?

• How would you feel to have such a quick and amazing response to your prayer?

Group 3

Read Jonah 2:1-3 to learn why Jonah was praying. Then read Jonah 2:10 to see how God answered Jonah's prayer.

Discuss the following questions with your group:

• What did Jonah pray about?

• How did God answer?

• How do you think Jonah felt about God's answer to his prayer?

Group 4

Read Exodus 2:23-24 to find out what the Israelite people were praying for, and then read Exodus 12:31-32, 40-41 to see how God answered them.

Discuss the following questions in your group:

• What did the Israelites pray that God would do?

• How did God answer?

• How long did the Israelites have to wait for God's answer? How do you think they felt during those many years?

Group 5

Read 2 Samuel 12:15-17 to find out what David prayed about. Then read 2 Samuel 12:18, 22-23 to find out how God answered David.

Discuss the following questions in your group:

• What was David asking God to do?

• How did God answer?

• How did David react to this answer from God?

Prayer Never Ends

"The Lord will hear when I call to him" (Psalm 4:3b).

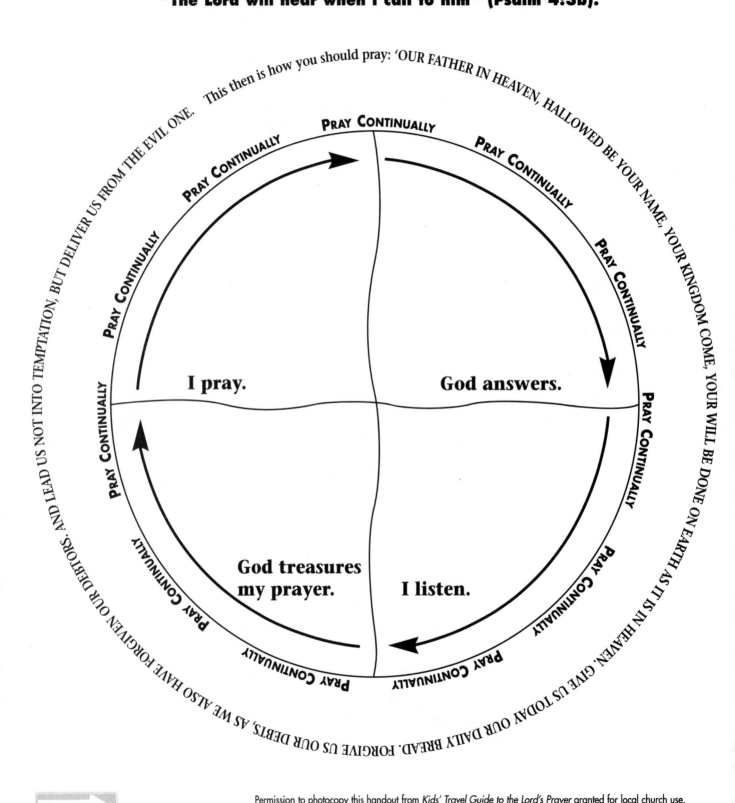

I pray.

God answers.

God treasures my prayer.

I listen.

(Around the circle: PRAY CONTINUALLY repeated; This then is how you should pray: 'OUR FATHER IN HEAVEN, HALLOWED BE YOUR NAME, YOUR KINGDOM COME, YOUR WILL BE DONE ON EARTH AS IT IS IN HEAVEN. GIVE US TODAY OUR DAILY BREAD. FORGIVE US OUR DEBTS, AS WE ALSO HAVE FORGIVEN OUR DEBTORS. AND LEAD US NOT INTO TEMPTATION, BUT DELIVER US FROM THE EVIL ONE.)

EVALUATION FOR

Kids' Travel Guide to the Lord's Prayer

Please help Group Publishing, Inc. continue to provide innovative and useful resources for ministry. Please take a moment to fill out this evaluation and mail or fax it to us. Thanks!

Group Publishing, Inc.
Attention: Product Development
P.O. Box 481
Loveland, CO 80539
Fax: (970) 679-4370

● ● ●

1. As a whole, this book has been (circle one)

not very helpful   *very helpful*

1   2   3   4   5   6   7   8   9   10

2. The best things about this book:

3. Ways this book could be improved:

4. Things I will change because of this book:

5. Other books I'd like to see Group publish in the future:

6. Would you be interested in field-testing future Group products and giving us your feedback? If so, please fill in the information below:

Name _____

Church Name _____

Denomination _____ Church Size_____

Church Address _____

City_____ State _____ ZIP _____

Church Phone _____

E-mail _____

Take children from K to 5th grade on a life-impacting adventure into the Fruit of the Spirit of Galatians 5:22-23. Engage them with activities, stories, prayer and much more. Children will learn all about the Fruit and about expressing God's love to others through caring actions, and healthy attitudes, with the help of God's Spirit.

Each of the 13 lessons includes:

Departure Prayer:

A time to prepare kids' hearts to receive Bible truths about Spirit Fruits!

First-Stop Discoveries:

Activity times to lead kids to see why the Fruit of the Spirit can help them live more loving, caring lives.

Story Excursions:

To bring the Fruit of the Spirit to life in fun, imaginative and dramatic ways.

Adventures in Living God's Laws:

Activities that show kids ways of living out the Fruit of the Spirit in their daily lives.

Souvenirs:

Kids create pages that go into a notebook to remind them of what they learned about God's laws. (Reproducible pages!)

Plus, *Tour Guide Tips* provide you help, and *Scenic Routes* provide even more creative options for your sessions.

Get in on the creative fun,
exploring the Fruit of the Spirit and how to live a more loving life!

ISBN 0-7644-2390-8 $16.99

Order today from your local Christian bookstore, order online at www.grouppublishing.com, or write:
Group Publishing, P.O. Box 485, Loveland, CO 80539-0485.

Kids' TRAVEL GUIDE to the 10 Commandments

Carol Mader

Get children into the Ten Commandments and the Ten
Commandments into their hearts in 13 easy lessons! Through
exciting journeys filled with stories, fun, prayer and adventure,
kids will learn that God gives us laws because he loves us!

ISBN 0-7644-2224-3 $16.99

Welcome to FaithWeaver Friends™!
See kids grow in faith, in
actions and in outreach!

FW Friends is a revolutionary midweek program that helps you see kids' real spiritual growth! Every week kids have a blast exploring God's Word and learning how to apply it to their lives. So you can watch them grow in Christ! You can use FW Friends as a midweek program or for Sunday school, an after-school program or anywhere you want kids to grow in faith, in actions and in outreach.

Everything about FW Friends emphasizes lasting spiritual growth. Kids begin at the Opening Celebration, separate to join their Circle of Friends as they rotate through Discovery Centers, take time for quiet reflection with their journals, then rejoin the other groups for the Closing Celebration.

FW Friends is easy and flexible. Every lesson and activity is clearly and visually laid out in several handy See-It Do-It™ leader guides. Any leader can actually sit down with a group of kids—See-It Do-It guide in hand—and lead them through any activity...with very little preparation needed!

FW stands for FaithWeaver™ and FW Friends is part of the FaithWeaver family of Christian growth resources. Contact us for more information about this family of resources that ties together Bible curriculum, children's church, midweek programming, and the home. FaithWeaver builds on the power of the family to encourage Christian growth.